NONFLICT

NONFLICT

The Art of
Everyday Peacemaking

AMIR KFIR, PhD
STEPHEN HECHT, MBA

Million Peacemakers

Authors contact information is:

Dr. Amir Kfir:
amirkfir@gmail.com
www.amirror.com

Stephen Hecht:
shecht@millionpeacemakers.org
www.millionpeacemakers.org

ISBN-13: 978-0-9950236-0-4

Cover Design: Alan Pranke
Illustrations: Pascal Bertrand
Cover photo: Alexandre Gauthier
using the Million Peacemaker's Advisory Board's hands

Printed in the United States of America

Contents

Introduction ix

Chapter 1. Conflict Basics 1

Chapter 2. Nonflict 21

Chapter 3. Step 1: Understand Yourself and Your Partner . .23

Chapter 4. Active Listening and Mirroring 37

Chapter 5. Step 2: Understand Your Shared Reality 47

Chapter 6. What Is Working Well for Us? 55

Chapter 7. Worst-Case Scenario 61

Chapter 8. Step 3: Co-Create .67

Chapter 9. Controllable Obstacles to Achieving
the Best-Case Scenario 77

Chapter 10. Overcoming Controllable Obstacles 81

Chapter 11. The Nonflict Way in Different Settings 87

Chapter 12. Preparation for Nonflict Discussions 99

Chapter 13. The Nonflict Way: A Brief Overview 103

Appendix. The Nonflict Way Cutout,
   Nonflict Worksheet.........................107

Addendum. Use of the Nonflict Way in Driving
   Social Change.............................117

The Nonflict Way in Business—Nonflict Forum........123

Power of Empathy.............................127

What's Next?................................131

Acknowledgments.............................133

Nonflict? In the two years it took to write this book, that one word that describes what happens to a conflict once it is resolved eluded us . . . until Nonflict. It was the pivotal moment, the excitement that we had finally succeeded in matching the outside-the-box thinking that conflict resolution so often requires with its name. We proudly present you with the new word we coined to express our concept . . . *Nonflict*®.

Introduction

Are you stressed over a conflict in your life? Will avoiding conflict make it go away? If you do try to avoid it, what if it gets worse? How do you get closer to your spouse who is angry about something you don't understand? It can be the same story with your kids. There even may be never-ending conflict at work, making the job more stressful than ever. How do you confront conflict without causing pain for yourself, your workplace, or people you care about?

We're confident that this book will offer answers to the questions above. By following our simple yet very powerful three-step process, the Nonflict way, you'll learn to recognize the real underlying conflict on both sides. You will then be able to resolve it together with your partner by co-creating, turning your conflict into a Nonflict.

We share our personal and other real-life examples, with exercises to help you easily apply conflict resolution concepts to your daily life. As you read, you will learn that conflicts are merely opportunities in disguise. You will learn how to use the Nonflict way for internal conflicts, two-person conflicts, group conflicts, and conflicts of a larger scale.

The Nonflict way is inspired by groundbreakers who came before us in the fields of conflict resolution, coaching, relationship therapy, positive psychology and change management. It is a result of our desire to help people find a constructive way of dealing with conflict, rather than following the destructive ones repeated from generation to generation—since the days of the caveman with a club. These days, we just have more effective "clubs."

Dr. Amir Kfir, an organizational psychologist since 1988, has counseled companies through various stages of conflict. As an Israeli who served in two wars, he has seen the cost of using force in conflicts and hopes his kids don't have to use force to resolve their country's conflicts going forward.

Stephen Hecht is a native Canadian who has experienced conflict on a different "battlefield." He is a successful businessman who has been active in the local, national, and international leadership of the world's leading network of CEOs—the Young Presidents' Organization (YPO). Over the course of more than three decades of working in private and public family businesses, Stephen has experienced many conflicts. Personally, he has experienced two divorces and three marriages, four kids, four stepkids, and many in-laws.

Stephen learned of Amir's conflict resolution successes in engaging YPO members of different groups—Greeks and Turks, Turks and Armenians, Israelis and Arabs, and American Jews and Muslims. Wanting to avoid repeating mistakes of his past and share these lessons with members of YPO Canada and the world at large, after Canada, Stephen asked Amir to help create an event that was later shared with over 700 CEOs, along with their spouses and young adult children. The event received amazing feedback—participants called it "life-altering"—and it also received YPO's "Best of Best" educational leadership development event internationally for 2012. The event's success led to requests to share it in other parts of the world—Africa, then Israel, Dubai, India, Mexico, Russia, the United States.

In August 2014, Stephen left his career in real estate to co-found– along with Amir and Frederic Latreille–an award-winning non-profit organization, Million Peacemakers. Its vision is a million peacemakers co-creating a culture of peace in the world by empowering people to transform conflict into Nonflict. With a focus on families, businesses, and communities around the world, along with a dedicated Advisory Board and strategic partners, Million Peacemakers is almost there and shows no sign of stopping at a million.

Million Peacemakers has trained people in over a dozen countries, ranging from Palestinians and Jews in the West Bank to First Nations in rural Canada to major corporate entities.

Success stories include Danone Waters in Spain which has used the Nonflict way to train their management with the goal of transforming diversity into an asset. They found it so effective they asked to translate the first edition of the book into Spanish to share Nonflict throughout their organization.

Sakal Media Group in India has started women's groups called Tanishka Forums, numbering over 120,000 women who are using the Nonflict way to effect positive change in their lives and communities. They also brought the training to

2,456 colleges through the Young Inspirators Network, effecting major change in the lives of thousands of young leaders and their communities as well.

The Tanishka forums are being duplicated in Mexico with the leadership of the Salinas Group who is also sharing the Nonflict way with children from troubled homes in a program called Sport is Your Gang. More details of these stories can be found in the Addendum.

Among the many people we worked with, we were not too surprised to learn how much business, personal and community conflicts have in common in all these places. Inspired by those lives we positively affected, we share this process with you.

The Structure of This Book

Each chapter of *Nonflict: The Art of Everyday Peacemaking* breaks down the three steps of the Nonflict way and explains the rationale and background of how to carry out these steps most effectively. Throughout the book, we provide "Key Points" that summarize important takeaways and help you remember important definitions and tips. In addition, exercises at the end of each chapter will help you to synthesize the way and apply it to your daily life. In the appendix, you will find worksheets that you can use for your discussions and keep track of action plans. There is also a one-page summarized version of the Nonflict way that you can copy to keep handy as the need arises.

Most people will pick up this book because they're struggling to resolve a difficult conflict with another person. If this sounds like you, after you've read this book, please consider sharing it with the person or people with whom you are engaged in conflict so you can both be on the same page. Most of the exercises in this book are suited for a pair. If sharing with a conflict partner isn't possible, try the exercises with someone who is uninvolved, like a close friend or family member. No matter with whom you practice, you both stand to benefit and learn.

A Note about Language

Throughout the book, we talk about the hypothetical conflict that you, the reader, is facing. We don't know your gender or the gender of the person with whom you're in conflict. Instead of writing "he/she," we use "he" and "she" interchangeably. We value gender equality, and whether we use "he" or "she," the pronoun is not intended to indicate only that specific gender.

Also, the use of "your partner" refers to the person with whom you are in conflict. This can be your life partner, your coworker, your friend, your neighbor, your child, or anyone else.

Chapter 1

Conflict Basics

The only difference between stumbling blocks and
stepping-stones is the way in which we use them.
—Adriana Doyle

The Inevitability of Conflict

We live in a society, a culture, in which conflict is seen as negative. In fact, we see the very fact that we are having a dispute as a sign of trouble in our relationships.

But this view misunderstands the nature of conflict and is damaging to our ability to make progress in our relationships and to grow as individuals. *A conflict is simply the existence of at least two contradictory interests, desires, ideas, styles, or perceptions that come into contact with each other.* Our world is a world of conflict. As we write this, there are an estimated 7.2 *billion* people living on Earth. Amazingly, it's extremely unlikely that any of them completely agree on their view of the world. Think about your own life: have you ever met any two people who *completely* agree on everything always? This speaks to the wonder and diversity of human beings.

Not only do relationships grow, but people do too. This means that a relationship that was previously without much conflict may see the number of issues rise. This is natural and shouldn't be shunned. Conflict is inevitable, and this book is about how to productively engage in conflict so that all sides can learn from the experience.

For now, though, we'll discuss different ways that people often engage in conflict, many times as a result of the misunderstanding that it is a battle rather than a team effort.

Real vs. Artificial Conflict

One of the simplest forms of conflict to deal with is also one of the most common; that is, conflict arising from miscommunication or, sadly, lack of communication altogether. It may appear to us that we are having a genuine conflict, but if we were to calmly and openly discuss the issue, we would see that the apparently *real* conflict is actually *artificial*.

Professor Aharon Kfir, Amir's father, who helped shape Israel's public administration, told us the following story:

> In 1870, a French soldier in Germany was taken as a prisoner of war. In the prison camp, it was extremely hard to survive, but the soldier believed that there was a beautiful girl waiting for him at home. This gave him the hope he needed to keep going. During his time in the camp, he had one friend with whom he shared his secret. By the end of the war, he and his friend had managed to survive. When they left on their respective journeys back home, his friend worried that the Frenchman might return home to find the girl with someone else. His friend decided to write a telegram to the

girl to warn her that the Frenchman was coming home. Meanwhile, the Frenchman's girl had been faithful and waiting for him the entire time. She received the telegram and started to clean the house and prepare dinner for the Frenchman. When the Frenchman arrived at the house, he looked through the window and saw the table set for two, with flowers and wine. Assuming the table was set for someone else, the Frenchman was overwhelmed with grief. He leapt into a nearby river, killing himself. The next day, when the Frenchman's body was discovered, the girl, too, was overtaken by grief and ended her life the very same way.

This story is obviously extreme in the results to which miscommunication led, but it illustrates problems that can arise. Imagine how the story would have ended if the Frenchman had had the presence of mind to simply knock on the door and greet his lover. But rather than joy, we have tragedy. The lesson to take from the story is obvious: Judging a situation on the surface level alone, rather than looking deeper, can lead to serious—even deadly—errors.

It's an essential part of resolving any conflict to get to the bottom of the issue. We must explore the depths of our conflicts and see what the underlying problems are, and whether they are genuine or artificial; this will not solve every conflict, but it will remove some false ones and is something with which we need to engage before further progress can be made.

It helps us take the time to communicate and build trust, thereby gaining a deeper understanding of our partner's interests, as well as our own. From there, we can clearly see whether the problem is real or fake.

To close, here's an example of an artificial conflict that is a bit less tragic than that of the Frenchman: Two chefs are fighting over the last lemon in a pantry. They're screaming at each other and (stupidly) waving their knives around. The restaurant manager runs in, terrified of bloodshed and mayhem in his kitchen. He cuts the lemon in half, giving each chef his 50 percent. Neither of them is very happy, and the manager asks what the issue was. It turned out that one chef needed the lemon rind for his recipe, and the other chef needed the lemon juice! Had they taken the time to understand each other's needs, they both could have had all of what they wanted. Thus, they experienced an artificial conflict that occurred only as a result of their lack of effective communication.

By contrast, if both cooks had needed the whole lemon, there would have been a real conflict—the topic of the rest of this chapter and much of the book.

Five Styles of Conflict Resolution

As you read this section, try to think about which style of conflict resolution you tend to engage in. The four main ways people resolve conflicts are *flee*, *force*, *fold*, and *fifty/fifty*. Each of these methods may seem right at various times. In the long run, however, none manages to resolve the conflict and instead creates more tensions and even hostility. This section explains these styles and their problems, and you will see why a fifth way, *co-create*, is usually the best option.

Flee

It's natural for many of us to avoid engaging with conflict when we think that talking about the problem will be uncomfortable or even make things worse. Maybe your spouse gets home from a long day's work, and it just doesn't feel like the right time to talk about the credit card bill or issues with the kids. Or maybe your boss is stressed because of high expenses, so you don't ask for that raise. Amir works with a family business where members of the family flee from potential conflicts for fear of saying things out of emotion that they may regret later. The problem is that unless you address the elephant in the room, the point of conflict will fester. Maybe the elephant is even invisible to the other person, so by the time you're so upset that you snap, the other person thinks you're acting irrationally. Snapping or blowing up makes the conflict worse and creates more problems. If we keep fleeing, eventually we will lose control and say things that we regret.

Stephen shares:

> During my marriage to my now second ex-wife, our respective daughters faced a conflict that escalated into a conflict between the whole family. Our two daughters had clashing personalities and constantly fought while living together. My then-wife understandably felt protective of her biological daughter and tried to take her side whenever she could. This pushed me to take my biological daughter's side. These fights were so explosive and emotionally exhausting that my wife and I eventually told the girls to try to avoid each other.

This tactic didn't work. We all felt like we were walking on eggshells. There was so much tension in the house that any little dispute would explode into a battle. I'd say that our inability to deal with conflict, even after my daughter had moved out, was one of the reasons that our marriage ended in divorce. Another reason was our own personality incompatibility and difficulty in understanding and dealing with it. An excellent psychologist suggested we take the Myers-Briggs and a marriage compatibility test, which had powerful insight. While I was dating my current and final wife, Naomi, I asked her to take it as well, and after seeing our high compatibility score, I certainly felt more comfortable to pursue the relationship further. (As you see, I'm still an optimist. See humanmetrics.com for the Myers-Briggs/Jung test, which is one of many available.)

This doesn't mean that you should talk about every little issue. For example, when you're just in a bad mood and something bothers you that normally wouldn't, it might be best just to calm yourself. But when you avoid discussing important issues, like in Stephen's case above, you miss an opportunity to improve your relationships, to gain better self-understanding, and to grow. We must embrace conflict so that we, and our situations, can improve. (And don't we all have room for improvement?)

We also aren't saying that you should rush into things. Sometimes a conflict is very emotional, and postponing the conversation is the best way to go. This gives you time to calm down, collect your thoughts, and figure out how you really feel about the problem. If you rush to fix the conflict in the heat of the moment, when you aren't actually prepared to do so, you might only deal with the surface issue and not the underlying problem, or you might say something that you regret. Delaying the conversation is fine, as long as you make sure to have it while the issues are still fresh for you and your partner.

Key Points

- Unresolved conflict continues to boil under the surface and in the end is more difficult to cope with.
- The fear of uncontrolled explosive words causes many to avoid the conflict.
- You miss out on an opportunity to grow personally and in your relationships when you flee from conflict, choosing not to deal with it at all.

2. Force

Another common way that many of us deal with conflict is by sheer force—trying to impose our will or point of view on others. This is why most people associate conflict with violence (the most direct kind of force). "Force," however, doesn't always mean physical force. It also can be verbal and psychological, or the use of power. Force might seem to be the quickest and easiest way to resolve conflicts, but it damages relationships and can lead to disaster in the long run.

Stephen shares:

> When I was running a clothing manufacturing company in Montreal, my unionized employees were dissatisfied with their wages and working hours, and they tried to force their demands through threat of strike. I could not afford to accept their proposal

because I knew our costs would go too high, and it would risk the survival of the company. I therefore had no choice but to say no. The workers then went on strike. They knew that they were in a powerful position and hoped that the strike would compel me to change my mind. The pressure was intense. On the one hand, I had very little prospect of being competitive with higher costs; on the other hand, we needed to produce goods. I looked around for other options. I thought about outsourcing the factory and found the solution in Korea. Shortly thereafter, we closed the Montreal factory, with the unfortunate result of leaving the employees unemployed. I was able to "win" because I changed the balance of power, but my "win" did not feel like winning, because it came at a cost to many long-term employees, who lost their jobs, and to me, in having to manage the quality and work of a factory thousands of miles away. There were no winners here, with both of us using force as a strategy.

Amir shares:

A friend of mine moved overseas to work for an international firm. His employment terms were based on a letter of intent with the employer. The compensation after a test year would be based on a percentage of billable work. After a year of performing extremely well, it was time to come back to finalize the next phase of their agreement. The employer then stated that although the letter of intent said one thing, it was not a binding commitment. In an argument around the interpretation of the original understanding, the employer very bluntly said: "Take it or leave it." He even said, "If you don't like it, you can pack your stuff and go back home." My friend understood in this moment that there was no alternative, and he had to accept what was laid out; he folded and submitted to the power imposed on him at that point. This display of *force* broke a bond of trust between the two. My friend felt this put a lot of stress on an otherwise complementary team. From that day forward, he was extremely cautious with any negotiations he made with his employer, and any negotiation about compensation and money turned out to be unhealthy and unnecessarily long because of the fundamental break in trust.

Key Points

- The idea that conflict has to have winners and losers can create feelings of alienation, bitterness, and even vindictiveness in the "losing" party.
- The world is constantly changing, and this means that power dynamics change too. A forceful resolution means there will be a loser; eventually, the conflict may resurface, as the loser has been pressured into agreeing to a conclusion he didn't want.
- The use of force also can be seen by many as immoral.

3. Fold

Both Amir and Stephen might be described as harmony seekers (why else would we write a book on conflict resolution?). We do everything we can to promote positivity in our personal and professional relationships. Sometimes this means that when we come into conflict with someone, we put our own interests aside for the sake of other people's interests. We pick our battles, and some just don't seem worth fighting, so we fold. Why risk the relationship?

But other reasons can lead to folding. You might fold when you think your partner is stronger, and you don't think that you have a chance to win by force. A simple example of this is in poker: Say I have no pairs and my opponent obviously has a good hand (she really is horrible at being straight-faced!).

Folding too often (outside of poker, at least) can give the impression that you can't stand up for yourself. This, in turn, can lead people to take advantage of you. Some other people might assume that if they're the ones giving in this time, their partners will return the favor in a future dispute. This assumption may be incorrect. It might make your partner feel more confident about her ability to win. There is no guarantee that anyone—not even a close friend—will understand what you have sacrificed by folding. Even if she does, there is no guarantee that she will remember this in the future and fulfill expectations that you haven't set.

Stephen shares:

> When I worked in a real estate company, it was essential that we sign a lease with a large tenant in order to develop land for a shopping center. This tenant dragged out the negotiation until the last

day of the option period on the land, which we couldn't extend, as there was another purchaser waiting to take our place. The tenant realized that he had this power over us and decided not to collaborate with us on an important clause. In this case, we decided to *fold* in order to keep the project. This caused us to feel a great deal of resentment toward this tenant, impacting our relationship, and we lost confidence in our partnership. The next time we needed a tenant, we changed our strategy by negotiating with his competitors as well.

Key Points

- As with force, folding promotes winners and losers. By sacrificing your own needs and desires, you encourage the notion that your needs and desires are less important than your partner's—which they aren't.
- If you fold, you may expect to be recognized and compensated for your generosity later in life. You may be disappointed, however, because not everyone follows this "rule."

4. Fifty/Fifty

Think way back to kindergarten. Do you remember when your teacher always told you what you should do with the toys? Share! From an early age, we're taught the importance of sharing. We're taught that we should give up on our desires so that we can make others happy. If you've got the coolest toy around and don't let your friends play with it, you're seen as selfish and unfair. Equality is important, but the conflict resolution equivalent of sharing—compromising—can cause problems.

We often compromise because we know that if we can't get everything we want, we can at least get part of it. It's fast, easy, and there's none of the embarrassment for either party that comes from fleeing, folding, or forcing. In fact, it seems like the perfect solution at first glance. Even so, compromising is similar to force, because the results are potentially unstable; each is satisfied that he has come to a midway agreement, but nobody's perfectly happy with the outcome. The shifting power dynamics mentioned when talking about force come into play here. Once power dynamics change, who is to say the compromise might not be reevaluated?

Amir shares:

> When my two kids were younger, they would fight over the TV in the living room. My daughter, who was older, wanted to watch different shows than her younger brother—she preferred *Friends*, and he wanted to watch *SpongeBob*. Their fighting got so bad that my wife and I had to intervene. We suggested that one could view TV in our bedroom, but that started another fight as to who had to leave the favored larger-screen living room TV. Finally, we said, "No TV for both of you until you stop fighting and figure this out." They then came up with a plan: He could use the living room TV one day, and she could use it the next, on an alternating schedule. Even though the fifty/fifty agreement was technically fair, both kids soon were unhappy with it. For example, they each still preferred the living room TV, and sometimes his favorite shows were airing on the day when she had control of that TV. Even worse, sometimes the bedroom TV

was not available (someone was actually sleeping in the bedroom), forcing one of the kids to watch the other kid's show in the living room. Or if he was out of the house and she used "his" TV time, he later would argue that he wanted more living room TV time to compensate. There were good days of sharing, but there also were days when one or the other was spiteful about not letting the other see a favorite show if it wasn't that person's assigned day. Fifty/fifty was too simplistic to satisfy both kids' needs over time. What ended up ultimately working well was the kids growing up and enjoying the same program together and becoming comfortable with a more harmonious flow during the day, allowing each other to see each other's favorite programs. Being able to watch TV on the computer was helpful too.

Key Points

Though fast and expedient, *fifty/fifty* often leads to two things:

- Both parties feel less than satisfied.
- Both parties compete to "one up" the other in order to change the power balance.

5. Co-Create

What's better than compromising? Co-creating, of course—you already know how to compromise, so why else would you bother reading the book? While co-creating might initially seem difficult—more difficult than the other four methods—it is the most fulfilling for everyone involved. It is especially important when we know we will have to continually deal in the future with the people with whom we're conflicting, since it helps to preserve and strengthen relationships. Co-creating considers the interests of each party, fully and equally.

Co-creating is based on the idea that there are an unlimited number of possible outcomes, and it supports the idea that two heads are better than one. Rather than each party working separately to achieve whatever is best for herself, each works together to achieve a solution that is, in fact, best for everyone. Co-creating leads to resolutions that are effective in the long term and help maintain—or create—healthy relationships.

Amir shares:

> I once was brought in to consult with a very large company that got into deep financial trouble. The CEO originally thought the fastest and simplest resolution was to *force* 10 percent of the company's workforce to leave the company. This decision would be quick and seemingly easy to implement with all the vice presidents, but it would create low morale among the employees and distrust in the leadership. Upon further thought, the CEO decided instead to cut salaries across the board, so everyone would sacrifice equally. His employees complained that this *fifty/fifty* move would not be an effective long-term resolution, because it would negatively impact some key functions and potentially cause the most valuable and marketable employees to leave. Out of desperation and fear of making the situation worse, the CEO decided to do nothing with the salaries and then chose to *flee*

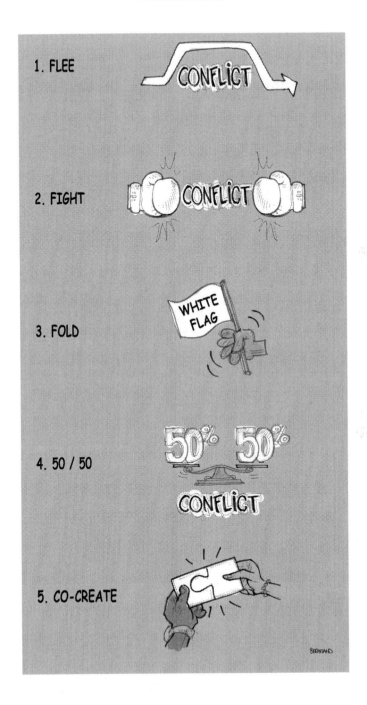

1. FLEE

2. FIGHT

3. FOLD

4. 50 / 50

5. CO-CREATE

the situation. By doing nothing, the company only took on more and more debt.

Finally, as we started to work with the leadership team as a group, we found a *co-created* solution. We invited the employees for an open-forum meeting, during which we received their feedback about their understanding of how the company needed to change in order to become more efficient, effective, and better aligned to deal with changes in the markets, and in doing so, also meet the needs of the employees for job security. In the end, the agreed-upon resolution was to reorganize certain functions and create new profit centers. We offered certain employees a transfer from non–revenue-generating functions of the company to revenue-generating ones. For example, employees in administration were retrained and shifted to production and sales. The employees were happy because they could keep working at the company and their salaries were not decreased. The leadership was happy because the company was able to produce more income and gain breathing space to deal with its debt problem. This restructuring returned the company to profitability and created a new culture of openness, participation, and trust, which could not have occurred using forcing, fleeing, or fifty/fifty to resolve the conflict.

Key Points

- When co-creating is used as conflict resolution, both parties are completely fulfilled in their needs and desires—a win/win situation.
- The resolution is long term, because no one feels overlooked or unaccounted for.

Here are more examples of co-created solutions to everyday problems:

Conflict

A husband and wife are arguing over what to do on their Saturday nights. The husband is more extroverted and would like to go out to parties with their friends. The wife is more introverted and would like to stay at home due to her discomfort in being around and having to socialize with large groups of people.

Co-Created Solution

The couple plans their Saturday nights together. Instead of going to a party or staying home, just the two of them, they go on double dates with other couples, allowing for better quality conversations, rather than superficial small talk in a large group. This allows the husband to socialize with others and allows the wife to have the type of conversations that make her feel content.

Conflict

A manager is angry with one of his employees who habitually arrives late. The employee apologizes and says that she has no control over when she gets to the office. She is a single mother and has to take her son to preschool in the mornings. Sometimes the carpool line at the preschool is long, and this makes her late for work.

Co-Created Solution

The manager and the employee discuss the situation openly. They agree that the employee will be able to enter the office late as long as she makes up the lost time during her lunch break. Through this resolution, the manager is satisfied because the other employees will see that the employee is respecting the office rules and not receiving special treatment, which might encourage others to come to work late. At the same time, the employee is able to see her son off to school every morning, which gives her the peace of mind that she needs to work well at the office.

Conflict

A husband and wife argue about family dinners. The husband thinks that it's very important that they have meals together to regularly check in with one another and regroup as a family, as he had when he grew up. The wife agrees with this sentiment, even though it wasn't the norm in her family, but she dislikes family dinners because this requires her to spend hours in the kitchen, preparing the meals.

Co-Created Solution

The family brainstorms how to have dinner together without putting the extra stress of meal preparation all on the wife's shoulders. They agree that the other family members will help with cooking the family dinners and the cleanup after. They agree to use innovative fast-meal cookbooks and include the option to eat their family dinner at a restaurant, with time to talk and enjoy each other fully.

Exercise

1. Your own conflict resolution style

Consider which conflict resolution style you most likely use. How has it worked for you? What impact has this had on you and your relationships?

BEFORE.   NOW.

BERTRAND

Chapter 2

Nonflict

O nce you take the time to consider the Nonflict way, it should seem clear and intuitive.

Step 1: Understand Yourself and Your Partner

- Share your view of the conflict. Ask yourself:
  What is the conflict? How does it make me feel?
  What is important for me?
- Your partner responds with the essence of what you have said and asks:
  Have I understood you well? Is there anything else?
  (You and your partner switch roles and repeat the questions above.)

Step 2: Understand Your Shared Reality

You and your partner discuss together, asking yourselves:
- *What is our real underlying conflict?*
- *What is working well for us?*
- *What is our worst-case scenario?* (Visualize facts and feelings.)

Step 3: Co-Create

You and your partner discuss together, asking yourselves:
- *What is our best-case scenario?* (Visualize facts and feelings.)
- *What are the obstacles to achieving our best-case scenario?*
- *What can we do to overcome controllable obstacles? Who will do what, when?*

Exercise

1. Current conflicts

Think about conflicts you are currently facing that you want to resolve. Have them in mind as you go through the book so that the lessons have immediate take-home value for you.

Chapter 3

Step 1: Understand Yourself and Your Partner

γνῶθι σεαυτόν *(Know yourself)*
—inscription written at the Temple of Apollo

*Before you step into someone else's shoes, remember
to take off your own.*
—Devan Capur, Entrepreneur

An enemy is a person whose story we have not heard.
—Gene Knudsen Hoffman, Author of
Compassionate Listening

The first step to co-create is to understand. You and your partner each share your own views of the conflict by answering the questions: *What is the conflict and how does it make me feel? What is important for me?*

Framing

Imagine that you are at an art museum with a friend, and you see an abstract painting. You insist that the painting is meant to represent a duck. Your friend, on the other hand, insists that it is a rabbit! The title of the painting is *Brick on a Sunny Day*, but the artist was clearly mistaken.

In everything we see and do, we are presented with data. Sights and sounds and thoughts and feelings all endlessly stream before us. Each of us is privy to the sights and sounds, which are common, but there are different ways to interpret them and on top of that, we then have our own thoughts and feelings about the sights and sounds (or more accurately, about our interpretations of the sights and sounds). We even have our own ways of perceiving, for example, a speech that is given. Say there is a politician shouting about a divisive political issue. Someone who disagrees with the politician is horrified by the speech and his presentation—the politician is shouting angrily, even like a lunatic! The supporter, on the other hand, hears the speech and almost is filled with tears by the passion that goes into it. Clearly, this is a great man who cares deeply about the cause.

Among other things, the way that we interpret the data with which are presented depends on the framework from which we are working.

In Step 1, you share your view of the conflict, which is heavily based on your framing. Framing is *a set of data that influences your interpretation of the world.* The data comes from:

- upbringing (the values on which your parents raised you, the examples your parents set for you, your family environment);
- culture;
- physical environment;
- formal education;
- life experiences;
- genetics; and
- your emotional and physical state at the time of the discussion (healthy/unhealthy, tired/awake, happy/sad, hungry/full, for example).

These data create mental filters through which we process the world.

Imagine you were in the produce section of a grocery store and saw an apple. As young children, we're taught by our parents and our teachers to identify this object as an apple. It's so ingrained in our understanding of the world that we don't hesitate to make this association. But what if you were born on a remote island where no apples were grown? If you were asked to identify this object, you might relate it to another fruit you know, but you certainly would not say "apple." This is because you see the object through your own framing.

We tend to forget framing in our day-to-day lives. We simply assume that when we are experiencing a scenario, there is a right and wrong interpretation of the information. (Obviously we have the right one.) We then might argue with people who disagree with the correct interpretation to get them to see the light. There are, however, multiple valid ways to interpret the information we are presented with.

Stephen shares:

When my Canadian company sought to create a business partnership with a Japanese company, I realized how much cultural background affects business practices. Whereas business negotiations in North America are usually quick and straightforward, dealing with facts and figures and concerned with not "wasting time," my negotiations in Japan took a more holistic approach. The Japanese focused on getting to know me as a person and building trust and respect. I spent five days in Japan, touring together and sharing many meals, drinks, and factory visits before the Japanese host agreed to the partnership, and this was just a few hours before I was scheduled to depart. I was patient and understanding of this custom, though a little stressed, and I can imagine that this drawn-out process might cause problems for other North American companies who have different expectations for business deals. Some negotiators stall until the deadline as a force/power tactic to get you to give more than you otherwise would, so that you do not go home empty-handed. That wasn't the case here, where we were either a "go" or "no-go" on a business partnership.

Co-creating involves accepting different views of the same situation and finding a resolution that accommodates and respects those different views.

Constructive Communication

In order for your partner to understand your messages in Step 1 clearly (and vice versa), you first need to equip yourself with skills that allow for constructive communication.

Constructive communication uses language that is non-judgmental. As simply as possible, express how you are feeling and thinking, without placing blame on the other person. Constructive communication usually starts with "I" statements, such as:

- "I feel . . ."
- "I think . . ."
- "I want . . ."
- "I need . . ."
- "It's important for me that I . . ."

Destructive communication involves language that seeks to evaluate, judge, and/or blame. Sometimes we blame our partner for how we are feeling—which is ultimately under our own control—or we assume that we understand how the other person is thinking or feeling. We evaluate our partner and try to convince him to see our "right" way. Here are some examples of destructive communication:

- "You made me feel . . ."
- "I feel _____ because you . . ."
- "You are _____" (name calling)
- "You think (or feel) . . ."
- "You should (should not) . . ."
- "If you _____, I will _____." (using fear, threats, and/or intimidation tactics)
- "Why did you do _____?" (attacking, forcing them to defend themselves)

In Step 1, you answer the questions, *What is the conflict and how does it make me feel? What is important for me?* State your answer in a nonjudgmental way by using constructive communication. The importance of this is demonstrated in the following example:

Stephen shares:

> My son, Alex, is an incredibly talented artist. From the time he was a toddler, he was always drawing and creating. A few years ago, Alex, was college-entry age. He was trying to decide what he wanted to pursue as a career. He was really keen on following a bachelor of fine arts program, but his mother and I were concerned that studying art would put him in a weak position to support himself financially. We pushed him to major in architecture instead, and he allowed himself to be convinced. School began, and he did not enjoy his studies. In fact, over the course of the next two years, it became more and more obvious how unhappy he was. The architecture program did not suit him at all. He failed most of his classes, and he eventually dropped out of school.

Now let's imagine that when Stephen first approached his son about this conflict, he used *destructive communication.* He may have sounded like this:

> *Alex, why did you drop out of school without telling us? How could you be this irresponsible and immature? After all that we've done to support you, you're willing to throw it all away? It's as if you don't even*

care about your future! I know you think that life is all
fun and games, but you should look at the big picture.
Your choices in college can impact your life forever.
We might have to think twice about funding you at
another college.

A breakdown of this statement:

- Stephen attacks Alex. ("Why did you drop out of school without telling us?")
- Stephen assumes what Alex is thinking. ("You're willing to throw it all away," "It's as if you don't even care about your future," and "I know you think that life is all fun and games.")
- Stephen calls Alex names—"irresponsible" and "immature."
- Stephen tells Alex what he should do. ("You should look at the big picture.")
- Stephen uses fear tactics to convince Alex of his perspective. ("Your choices in college can impact your life forever" and "We might have to think twice about funding you at another college.")

How do you imagine Alex would have responded to this type of communication? Because Alex isn't a Buddhist monk, he probably would have responded in an equally destructive way. He would have felt hurt and become defensive. He might have insulted his father and accused him of thinking and feeling certain ways. Alex would have naturally engaged in the battle that his father started.

In reality, after learning from a few previous destructive conflicts, Stephen approached his son using *constructive communication*. He said something like this:

Alex, I want to talk to you because I love you, and I feel concerned for you. I'm worried that your behavior in school could get you in trouble in the future, and I don't want anything bad to happen to you. I also want you to be happy in your life and work in something that brings you joy. It would be helpful if I could understand what you're thinking and feeling. Can you please explain it to me?

A breakdown of Stephen's statement:

* "I feel"
* "I want"
* "I don't want"

Of course, Alex had a positive reaction to this statement. He was able to see that Stephen was coming from a place of love, rather than a place of moralizing judgment. He also felt comfortable opening up about his problems because he understood clearly how his father was feeling and thinking. If you're curious, Alex went on to pursue art with his parents' support, graduated college, and now is creating and selling beautiful paintings. He's also pursuing further education in art therapy to work with the elderly.

Self-Awareness, Honesty, and Vulnerability

Explaining the conflict from our perspective isn't always an easy task: it requires getting in touch with our emotions and becoming self-aware, something many of us dread! Sometimes this requires us to think about the situation privately before starting the discussion with our partner (the exercises at the end of this chapter can help with this). This is encouraged as long as the conversation is planned for and not delayed indefinitely. Thinking about and understanding yourself can be challenging, but if you practice self-awareness daily, it will become easier and more automatic. Moreover, self-understanding is essential for progress in this world. Just as a mechanic can't fix a car without examining it, we can't change ourselves without understanding where and who we are.

Some of us understand ourselves quite well but we're afraid of being honest and vulnerable with others. We fear their judgment or assume that they won't be able to understand us. In a perfect world, incorporating constructive communication with your partner from the beginning of the relationship would lessen fears you might have about receiving harsh judgment. We live, however, in the real world and sometimes feel blocked by the way we've always spoken with our partner. Making changes takes patience and practice. The sooner you begin, the sooner the benefits of using constructive communication will be felt.

Thinking that others don't have the capacity to understand is a common but baseless fear. Humans have a large capacity to empathize with numerous situations and feelings, even ones that they haven't experienced personally. Whether or not we voice this ability to empathize is another story; we will deal with the topic of empathy in the next chapter. Being honest and open with your partner is the only way to ensure that your needs will be met. If you can't communicate clearly what you want or need, how can you expect your partner to understand? Just as you aren't a mind reader, neither is he.

Amir shares:

Once I was on vacation with my wife in Puerto Rico. We were staying in a beautiful house on the beach. In the beginning of the trip, we spent every day relaxing on the sand, soaking up the sun, but eventually my wife got bored. She prefers to spend vacations in the midst of cities, wandering around, shopping, and trying to get a sense of the everyday hustle and bustle. When she asked me if we could go into the city to explore, I said yes without voicing that I would prefer to stay on the beach. (I just wanted to make her happy.) When we went into the city, I quickly became cranky and frustrated with all the stress and commotion. I started to resent my wife for bringing me there when I could have been sitting on a pristine beach with a margarita in my hand. My wife became aware of my negative energy and became equally frustrated. She asked me why I was acting so miserable when I had agreed that going to the city was a good idea. I told her that I preferred to be at the beach but I also wanted to make sure she was having a good time. It turned out that had my wife known that I was going to be unhappy, she would have chosen to go to the city alone.

This incident shows how important it is to express your needs and desires. You should never assume that your partner knows these feelings or feels the same way—every person has different needs and desires. Sometimes we learn them through trial and error, but the easiest and most straightforward way to learn them is to listen and hear what they are.

Part of the difficulty of the above situation was that Amir didn't realize that he'd dislike the city so much. He might have been able to recognize this and better deal with this if he'd been more self-aware about the types of environments that make him feel stressed and uncomfortable. In Step 1, we ask you to answer, *What is important for me*, to give you a chance to reflect on your needs and desires and express them clearly and openly.

It's hard to be completely honest and vulnerable when you're unaware of your own thoughts and feelings. This book's appendix offers a worksheet that gives you space to brainstorm and write down your view of a conflict before you express it to your partner.

Key Points

- An individual's personal framing determines how she views a particular situation or conflict.
- The existence of framing teaches us that in communication, we should seek not a resolution that labels someone "right" and someone "wrong"; it should be a resolution that takes into account all relevant perspectives.
- Constructive communication uses simple "I" statements without blaming or shaming your partner.
- Self-awareness and the ability to be honest and vulnerable with your partner are key elements in ensuring that your needs in any discussion are met.

Exercises

1. In the Other Person's Shoes

Think of the person with whom you're in conflict, and answer the following questions about him:

- What's his background and upbringing? How did his family deal with conflict?
- What's his work background and experience?
- In what culture was he raised, and how might this impact how he perceives the world today?
- What was his emotional state at the time of the argument? How might that have impacted the conversation?
- What other factors might have impacted the discussion?

Write these questions down on paper, and then try to answer them as if you were your partner. Then, with your notes in front of you, think of how you would describe the conflict if you were in your partner's shoes.

If you don't know the answers to the questions above, maybe it's a good time to get to know your partner more deeply. It will probably help you to understand his perspective on the conflict.

2. Getting to Know Yourself

If you're having trouble making sense of your own thoughts and feelings toward a particular conflict, try to answer the following questions. Think about how your upbringing may have impacted your attitude toward conflict today:

- How did your parents and siblings manage conflict while you were growing up? Do you think the method they used was positive or negative?

- Which of your or your family's behaviors did you want to repeat, and which did you vow never to repeat? Have you repeated those behaviors that you vowed never to repeat?

3. **Answering the Questions in Step 1** (What is the conflict and how does it make me feel? What is important for me?)

- **Crafting Your Response**

  When trying to answer the questions in Step 1, imagine your initial gut reaction. If you could say anything to that person, without fear of her reaction, what would you say? Would you accuse him of doing something? Would you call her nasty names? Write down this authentic response, and underline where you used destructive communication in your written response. Then try to rewrite your statement to the person using constructive communication as learned in this chapter.

- **Practice Makes Perfect**

  Imagine that you're standing in front of your partner with your constructive communication statement. What parts of that statement would be difficult to say in front of your partner? Which words expose your fears or insecurities? Practice saying those words in front of a mirror as you look yourself in the eye. Next, close your eyes and visualize yourself saying these words in front of your partner. Continue this practice until the action becomes comfortable.

 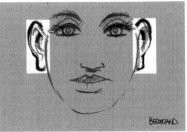

Chapter 4

Active Listening and Mirroring

Every person in this life has something to teach
me—and as soon as I accept that,
I open myself to truly listening.
—Catherine Doucette

To truly listen is to risk being changed forever.
—Sakej Henderson

The second part of understanding yourself and your partner is mirroring. Your partner mirrors the essence of what you've said and asks, *"Did I understand you well? Is there anything else?"*

Active Listening

Often what we call conversations are not, in fact, conversations. They are just people speaking to each other. A conversation requires the listener to listen *actively*, rather than taking the time while the speaker is speaking to think of what he himself is going to say when his turn comes, or even worse, interrupting because what he has thought of is so important!

A good active listener will not think of his or her own thoughts while the conversational partner is speaking but will listen and think about what the partner is saying and maybe think of questions to ask so that he or she can get a better understanding of what the speaker is trying to say.

To actively listen, you also have to free yourself from judgment, distraction, and expectation. You must pay full attention to what is being said, listening with a fully open mind. Maintaining eye contact when your partner is speaking to you is also critical. Even if you ultimately disagree, you should listen with the willingness to do so. Surely the speaker believes what she is saying for a reason; try to understand what that reason is—put yourself in her shoes.

It's not, however, just about what is said; it's about the whole process of communication, including verbal and non-verbal cues. You must pay careful attention to these things, on top of what is said explicitly.

When you or your partner do share facts and feelings, it's important not to dump so much at a time that it overwhelms the other's ability to process the information. It may be best to share one main "paragraph" at a time, allow the partner to mirror, and then continue. The flow will be more natural this way and provide the positive experience of sharing, listening, and mirroring throughout this step.

Stephen shares:

When I was working in a real estate company, I went to meet a potential client from whom we hoped to purchase land. When I walked into the room, the client had her arms crossed and was frowning. In an aggressive tone, she quickly told me that I must buy the property outright without our desired due diligence period; I could not drag her along for a year, like the last person who was interested in purchasing had done. Instead of defending my position, I tried to listen carefully. It was clear to me that she was hurt and frustrated from being manipulated and wanted to protect herself from being taken advantage of again. She did not explicitly tell me this, but it was implied by her tone and body language. Through active listening, I was able to understand what was important for her, and I was able to approach the conversation in a way that made her feel respected and safe (for instance, I told her about our 95 percent success rate and that we shared the same interests in that we could only develop the land if we bought it from her). In the end, we were able to strike a deal that was satisfying for both of us.

While your partner is expressing his view of the conflict, try to actively listen to *all* the messages he is giving. Only through active listening will you be able to mirror the essence of what your partner has expressed.

Mirroring

Mirroring means reflecting back the messages that you've understood from your partner. When you mirror what's been expressed, you don't repeat the exact words that your partner used. Rather, you try to capture the essence of what he has expressed by paraphrasing the words, emotions, body language, and tone.

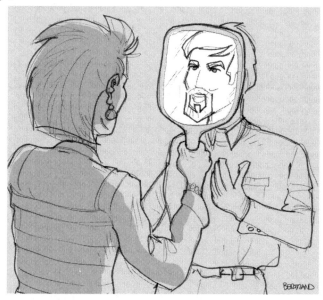

The mirroring technique is practiced in Imago therapy, a highly respected couples therapy that's been used throughout the world for over three decades. Harville Hendrix, the father of Imago therapy, teaches that mirroring forces us to practice active listening. When you're aware from the beginning that you will be expected to mirror what your partner is saying, you focus your entire attention on her message, instead of what's going through your own mind. (To help you focus on your partner's messages and not on those in your mind, you may wish to use the worksheet in the appendix to take notes while your partner is speaking—but not at the expense of eye contact.)

For good mirroring, it's necessary to grasp not only the spoken messages but also the emotional messages that your partner conveys, so you must be empathetic while listening.

Empathy

Have you ever been to the wedding of a distant relative or minor acquaintance but somehow found yourself tearing up during the ceremony? Or watched a reality show and cringed at the sight of people eating bugs? You might not have any emotional connection to the couple at the wedding, and you probably have never eaten bugs, but you can still imagine what those people were experiencing. That's because humans have a massive capacity to empathize.

Recent studies have shown that our wiring actually enables empathy. Neuroscientists who study mirror neurons note that the same cells are activated when we experience something ourselves as when we watch someone else experience the same thing. For example, these mirror cells are activated when you prick yourself with a needle *and* when a needle pricks someone else. This has huge implications for conflict resolution—mainly that we, as humans, can empathize with anyone, even when we feel animosity or hate toward that person.

Amir shares:

I once facilitated a meeting between Israelis and Arabs about their conflict. At one point, an Arab member of the group told us that his mother still held the key to the house she had to quickly leave in 1948 (during Israel's Independence War). He said she still held on to the dream of returning and living in that house. I was deeply touched by his story, and I tried to mirror back to him what he had said. I told him that I heard his pain, and I realized the deep trauma his mother must have experienced. I said that I could not imagine how I would feel if I needed to run away from home and was then prevented from returning for decades. I said that I would be dreaming of returning as well. When the Arab member heard me empathize with him and understand his pain, he became emotional. I didn't understand why he reacted that way, so I asked him what had happened. He replied that he never could have imagined an Israeli ex-paratrooper showing sensitivity to his family's tragedy and validating his reaction as normal. This became a turning point in our work together and in our desire to reconcile our pasts to build a better future.

By mirroring, you basically put yourself in your partner's shoes. As you speak, pay attention to how you present the information to your partner and try to do so in an empathic, non-judgmental way. Keep friendly, easy eye contact, and monitor your tone so that it's even, calm, and respectful (not mocking!).

You may be surprised by how easily you're able to mirror those with whom you're in conflict; just try it.

Validation

Another reason that mirroring is critical is that it makes your partner feel heard, understood, and *validated*. Often, conversations become fights because one or more persons feel they are not being fully heard. We shout or repeat ourselves to be recognized because acceptance and validation are common human needs (they fall under "esteem" on Maslow's hierarchy).

Mirroring eliminates any doubt in our mind that our partner may not be listening, so it keeps the conversation calm and collected. Through mirroring, we are able to legitimize our partner's point of view without necessarily agreeing with it. Validation helps us feel that our reaction is normal.

Stephen shares:

Recently, I was pulled over by a policeman for not making a complete stop at a stop sign and not putting on my turn signal before making a turn. Once pulled over safely, I turned off the engine and put my hands on the wheel so he could see I respected him and was not a threat. When the policeman approached me, I could tell he was very angry. Before he started speaking, I removed my sunglasses and tried to make direct eye contact. His first questions were, "Do you realize that you did not stop completely at that stop sign and did not use a turn signal as you turned right? Do you realize those are two infractions that give you two tickets and demerit points on your license?" After he finished speaking, I tried to mirror back the essence of his message and said, "You're right. I didn't stop properly and make a signal. That's really dangerous, and I definitely should have known better." At this point, his mood changed entirely. He suddenly became much calmer. He then said that he was concerned because this was a residential area, and there were children playing in the street. I mirrored him again by saying, "Yes, you're right. There are children in this area, and what I did was very dangerous. I definitely have to be more careful in the future." The policeman let me off with only a warning.

The questions that you ask after mirroring—*Did I understand you well? Is there anything else?*—serve as a double-check for validation. They give your partner a chance to clarify anything that you misinterpreted or forgot to include. Once feeling validated, it also gives her a chance to dig deeper as to what the real underlying conflict is, versus what may be its symptoms. If your partner says you didn't understand her, ask your partner to clarify. You or your partner should *never* say, "Yes, you understood me well," just for the sake of being conciliatory. Part of a constructive conflict resolution is practicing clear and honest communication—this means being honest with your partner, even if it risks hurting her feelings. Honesty is the foundation of mutual trust and respect, so sugarcoating issues doesn't even give the relationship a chance for success.

Key Points

- Mirroring depends on active listening. Pay attention to your partner's words, emotions, body language, and tone.
- Mirroring means paraphrasing, not repeating word for word, and capturing the essence at the deepest level.
- Mirroring requires empathy. Put your ego aside and step into the shoes of your partner, which then comes out in your respectful tone and body language.
- We humans have a large capacity to empathize with others, no matter how angry we may be.
- Mirroring leads to validation, which communicates to the other person that thinking and feeling as they do is not totally unreasonable. Validation builds trust and helps your partner to open up to you.

Exercises

1. Active Listening with a Closed Mouth

To practice active listening, sit with a partner and ask him to talk to you about an issue in his life that is troubling him deeply. Let your partner speak for two minutes without interruption. Monitor your responses to this person.

- Are you able to keep eye contact with your partner for the entire two minutes?
- Are you able to stop yourself from interrupting him?
- Do you allow yourself to empathize with him?
- Are you paying attention to your own thoughts or to what your partner is communicating?

2. Mirror, Mirror on the Wall

To practice mirroring, take turns with your partner answering one of the following questions:

- What is one day in your life that you would love to live again and why?
- Who is a person who has had a major impact on your life and why?
- What are you most thankful for?
- What event was a major turning point in your life and why?

The nonspeaking partner should then mirror the essence of the facts and feelings of the speaking partner while using a nonjudgmental tone.

3. Empathizing with the "Other"

To practice empathy, sit with a partner with whom you are *not* in conflict.

- Explain the conflict from your perspective to your noninvolved partner.
- Your partner then mirrors back to you what you have expressed.
- Next, physically switch seats with your partner, take off your own shoes, and role-play as if in the shoes of the person with whom you are in conflict. Explain the conflict and the feelings from that person's perspective, as you imagine it.
- Your partner mirrors again what you have expressed.

In this exercise, your partner is not a player in the conversation but an important vehicle for you to hear and understand your own position and the position of the other person in the conflict (who might not be present). Although taking the role of your "other" may seem uncomfortable at first, the ability to get inside that person's head and imagine the words he would use will help you to understand him better.

Chapter 5

Step 2: Understand Your Shared Reality

*Don't be afraid of opposition. Remember, a kite
rises against, not with, the wind.*
—Hamilton Mabie, essayist, editor,
and lecturer

What Is Our Real, Underlying Conflict?

In Step 2, we shift from viewing the situation as individuals to viewing the situation as a team with a common conflict.

The underlying conflict is that which unites both perspectives. For example, let's say that you're sick of your coworker, who sits in a cubicle next to you. You might describe the situation as, "All day, he can't shut up while on the phone with clients, and he's so loud and obnoxious that I can't even hear myself think! If I had it my way, I'd work in a library. Better yet, he'd quit." The underlying conflict, however, seems to be respect or patience with different work styles or a difference of personalities. After all, he is on the phone with clients, so surely he's working.

Identifying the underlying conflict not only helps you to focus on an effective resolution, but it also separates the individual from the conflict. The conflict is not really about your coworker and how difficult a person he is; it's about the conflicting differences in how you work. Does this mean that one of you is working the right way and the other is working the wrong way? Certainly not. Conflict doesn't have to create winners and losers—two equally rational people can have conflict, and their differences of opinion or style can be equally valid. Part of the joy (and the challenge) of the human experience is learning how others act and perceive things differently so that we can open our horizons and possibly modify our own ways for the betterment of all involved. Wouldn't it be a boring life if we remained unchanged throughout?

Here is a list of common conflicts between two people:

- Different work styles
- Different values/priorities/needs (e.g., money, charity, diet, sex)
- Different communication styles
- Different conflict resolution styles
- Different views of cleanliness/orderliness
- Different views of punctuality
- Different sleep patterns
- Different personalities
- Different levels of anxiety and calmness

Causes vs. Symptoms

One significant challenge with identifying the real underlying conflict is that we have a tendency to talk about the symptoms instead of the causes. Every conflict can be divided into causes, symptoms, and results. (We'll ignore results for now, because they will change after we find a resolution.) The causes are the basic elements of the real underlying conflict. Symptoms, by contrast, are merely the more obvious, surface-level problems. If we confuse a symptom with a cause, we risk encountering the same conflict over and over again because we will not have addressed the core of the issue during the resolution. This can actually lead to more extreme (negative!) consequences in the long run.

For example, a mother brings her son to the doctor with an ear infection. The boy is crying and seems to have a lot of pain in his ear. The doctor has medication that can lessen the pain for the boy. The pain, in this case, is the symptom. The danger in only treating the symptom is that you lose sight of the real underlying problem: an ear infection that caused the pain in the first place. There is a risk that in only treating the pain, the ear infection will never be treated, and this could lead to irreversible hearing damage (result). A doctor might offer the pain reliever, but would first gather all the information she can about the symptoms and potential causes before making a diagnosis and plan for treatment.

Amir shares:

> During the last six months of my military service, I worked on a special training program for kids from low-income families who had been raised under really tough conditions. Some of them had criminal backgrounds and were involved in gang violence. The government wanted to give them another chance by integrating them into society, using military discipline, culture, and skill learning to do so. Instead of merely handing these kids a uniform and letting them fend for themselves, my

commanders and I built a program for them that took a holistic approach.

First, we asked a social worker to visit with their families. This helped us to understand the problems that many of the kids were facing with poverty, violence, and drugs. With this information, we knew we had to find a way to help these kids gain positive self-esteem and hope for their futures. We decided that by teaching them valuable skills that they could use in careers outside of the military, they could start to see the positives in taking responsibility for their own lives and in behaving differently. We have learned that the deep meaning of the word *responsibility* is the ability to respond in a responsible manner.

If we had approached these kids from a superficial level and merely taught them the basics of military training, it would not have addressed the root of the problem. These kids likely would have picked fights on the first day and been thrown in jail. By investigating and truly listening, we discovered that these kids were not bad kids but merely were products of their environment, and this is what helped us to help them. The key to our relative success was helping these young men develop self-esteem.

Stephen shares:

When I was in the formalwear business, I had one store in a chain of stores that had lower sales week after week. I asked myself why this store was doing more poorly than the others. Some of my associates claimed that the economy was poor in the area where the store was located, so people were spending less on formalwear. I decided to take a closer look and investigate the situation myself by making a surprise visit to the store. When I got there, I noticed that the store looked messy and unprofessional. This was very disturbing, especially since we prided ourselves on being organized and clean. This caused me to look deeper—how could this be? Was the manager alone to blame? Was there an employee who had not cleaned up after a busy period the night before? Was it always messy or just this once? I could have stopped there and said that the poor upkeep of the store was why it was losing money. Instead, I had to keep digging. I asked for the employee shift schedule and headed to check the inventory in the back room. The inventory was also disorganized. I had a very bad feeling of what was to come. After spending some time in searching, I discovered—in a corner, under a pile of random items in the backroom—a shoebox full of cash. From that moment, it did not take long to conclude that the manager of that store was actually stealing a portion of the sales. That was the real problem, while the appearance of the store was just a symptom of poor management.

When you are having difficulty moving past a symptom, always ask, "Why?" and the cause will necessarily be the answer. Sometimes it takes more than one round of asking why—both for your partner and for you—for this to work. For example, if your friend isn't talking to you, ask yourself why. If your answer is that she is upset with you, ask why again. Most symptoms are derivative of something deeper going on in each individual's conscious or unconscious memory. The cause could even be a result of a memory of pain with a different person from his past that was triggered by something that occurred in the present with the two of you. For example, with a married couple, an act of betrayal ten years ago by an ex-spouse or even a parent's affair might put into context a conflict the couple is having today with trust and intimacy.

The cause could also be influenced by a difference in your or your partner's personal beliefs. If you believe women should stay at home to raise children and your partner believes women should have a traditional career, even with children, this difference in beliefs would likely be the cause of a conflict when you have children together.

Sometimes you'll learn that the deeper cause in an interpersonal conflict is related to an internal conflict you're facing. This internal conflict may need to be dealt with before interpersonal work can be done. (Chapter 11 shows how to use the Nonflict way to help work through internal conflicts.) Many complex issues can be simplified or resolved once we work on ourselves first.

Key Points

- Don't get bogged down in specific actions or people. Focus on the total, all-encompassing issue.
- Ask yourself, *"Why are these two equally valid perspectives clashing?"*
- Discern the symptoms from the real underlying causes to the conflict.

Exercise

Write down some of your beliefs that you think may be influencing the conflicts in your life. What are your beliefs about the role of men and women, success, marriage, God, money, power, and work? What do you think your partner's beliefs are on the issues over which you are in conflict?

Chapter 6

What Is Working Well for Us?

A pessimist sees difficulty in every opportunity;
an optimist sees opportunity in every difficulty.
—Winston Churchill

Positive Psychology

People in conflict often only consider the negative aspects of their relationship with the individual with whom they're in conflict. They forget the beneficial, or positive, aspects of their relationship. Before you dive into resolving the conflict, it's essential that you reflect on what *is* going well in the relationship and what you appreciate about those things. It's also important to include not only the facts but the feelings as well. (This point comes from a field of study called Appreciative Inquiry.) It's unlikely that your relationship is *completely* bad. In the worst case, maybe the only thing that's working well is that both parties want to resolve the conflict; this is, however, enough. When you discuss positive aspects of the relationship, you remind each other why the relationship is valuable, and it helps the conversation progress in a constructive direction.

If you can't think of *anything* positive about the relationship or the other person, you can at least be thankful for the conflict you're experiencing. This conflict has brought you together, and it has the potential to help you grow in unimaginable ways. It's your avenue to learn about each other's differences and find ways to celebrate and utilize them; if you follow the Nonflict way, you'll grow individually as well as interpersonally.

Conflicts are extremely important for companies because managing conflicts correctly can prevent major destructive conflicts down the road. Therefore, conflicts ought to be seen as opportunities for growth and continuous improvement, rather than as things that hold the company back.

We've witnessed the power of this grounding question—what is working well for us?—in numerous discussions with families, coworkers, and even embittered enemies. It's always easy to point out people's faults, especially those of people close to us, but when a married couple in conflict can step back and realize that they actually have an amazing family, and that they were able to raise great kids together, a new energy is created around the discussion. Or when a parent stops to think about her child, who, even though he's getting into trouble in school, has a tremendous heart and is a friend to everyone, she can use this positivity to keep her motivated toward working on a resolution.

Amir shares:

> I work with McElroy, an American-based world-leading manufacturing company that designs, builds, and markets specialty construction equipment. Their products are sold almost exclusively through distribution, and as such, they work with many distributors around the world. One of their

larger distributors evolved their own business model away from the *sale* of their products to that of an equipment *rental* model with nationwide coverage. McElroy's business model and their customer's business model had migrated away from each other. Instead of ending the business relationship with this distributor, McElroy executives sat down with representatives from the distributor to understand each other's business models and aspirations. Because they valued the importance of this working relationship and how it had benefitted each of them in the past, and they could see how their vision for the future would also be mutually beneficial, they worked to create resolution by developing a new market channel arrangement. This new market channel option was then made available to all their distributors and helped fuel further growth with other strategic partners.

By remaining engaged in the dialogue and working to understand the other side's needs and aspirations, a solution emerged that not only saved an important customer but was offered to other partners in the future to great benefit to McElroy and their distributors.

Many findings in the field of positive psychology support the power of remaining optimistic in your discussions. Martin Seligman, psychologist and author of *Authentic Happiness*, claims that if you approach problems with a positive outlook, you're more likely to reach a positive result. Prof. Tal Ben-Shahar, another big name in positive psychology, from Harvard, teaches that people who keep a "gratitude journal"—who each night before going to sleep write at least five things for which they are grateful—are happier, more optimistic, more successful, and more likely to achieve their goals. But these aren't just claims; Shawn Achor's *The Happiness Advantage* indicates that the data clearly supports the idea that a happy disposition improves productivity, creativity, and overall success (even on tests!).

In interviewing forty of the world's most successful business executives, Jeffrey Garten, dean of the Yale School of Management, found that the one trait that united them all was optimism. He says that while most of us assume that the most successful people are extremely aggressive in negotiations, the opposite seems to be true. "Their view was, I know I have succeeded in the past, and I'm quite confident that if I can look beyond today's problems to a point on the horizon, I know I'm going to get there." When working through your own conflicts, always remain confident that you can resolve the issue by looking at the larger picture. In any situation, some things are still worth appreciating.

Stephen shares:

> A member of the Young Presidents' Organization, who attended one of our conflict-resolution trainings, contacted me six months later to tell me a story about a conflict between his wife and daughter. His wife and daughter had not spoken to each other for months, due to misunderstandings and frustrations related to the daughter's spell with depression, which had caused her to struggle with staying in school. He and his wife took their daughter to visit a new school that might be better suited for their daughter's needs. During the car ride back, his daughter and wife broke their silence in an explosive, emotional argument. He pulled over

the car and used the Nonflict way to help his family calm down and have a constructive conversation. He said that their saving grace was when his wife and daughter stopped to think about the positives in their relationship, the feeling of love they had for each other, and that they wanted the best for each other. His daughter, who was in a really dark place, needed that reminder of why working with her mom to better their relationship was important.

Key Points

- "What is working well for us" means *what is working well for our relationship and what do I appreciate about the other person?—This should include facts and feelings.*
- Maybe the only thing that's working well is that both parties want to resolve the conflict; you can still recognize this.
- Thank the universe for your conflict.
- Research has shown that positive discussions yield positive results.

Exercises

1. Practicing Positive Psychology

Make a list of at least three things that are going well in your personal life (your physical, mental, and emotional well-being), your family life, and your work life. Share this list with your partner. Keep this list where you can see it, like on the bathroom mirror or the refrigerator.

2. Gratitude Journal

Many psychology studies have shown the positive impact on individual happiness of keeping a journal in which you record what you are grateful for on a regular basis. This works best if you write before you go to sleep, daily or at least three times a week. Try it yourself to see the power of this simple task.

Chapter 7

Worst-Case Scenario

*Courage is not the lack of fear but the
ability to face it.*
—John B. Putnam, publisher

*Everything that scares you is an opportunity
to know your best self better.*
—Robin Sharma, author

Facing Our Fears

Every morning, a Buddhist monk juggled a crystal ball, tossing it from one hand to the other. One morning, a student discovered the monk during his morning ritual and asked the monk why he wasn't scared about dropping the crystal ball and shattering it. The monk replied, "In my mind, it already fell. Now I'm just enjoying it."

Imagining and experiencing the worst facts and feelings can actually free our minds to look at things more positively. Once we confront the worst-case scenario and we see that it's something with which we can live, we can move on with our lives and live more practically. No longer are we caught up in paranoia, and we can take the next steps toward improvement.

On the other hand, if the worst case for the parties involved is truly disastrous, the perceived crisis could be the catalyst needed to work on a resolution, with the Nonflict way to guide you.

Amir shares:

> I have a good friend, Yoki Gil, whose business, named Source Vagabond, is a world leader in hydration systems, hiking sandals, and travel accessories. His competitors continually stole his intellectual property. This situation forced him into numerous legal cases around the world, which took up his time and money. He felt passionate about fighting for his rights, but he also realized that the court cases left him exhausted, and the only ones who won in court were the lawyers. As he told me his story, I asked him, "What is the worst that could happen if you don't take these competitors to court?" He said, "They could steal my ideas and profit from them. They could take everything I've created over the last twenty-five years and compromise my position in the international market, and other competitors will feel free to do the same."

When I mirrored these fears back to him, he was able to examine them outside of himself in a calm, constructive manner. Soon, he realized that even though he was actually living his worst-case scenario emotionally, there was a way around it. Instead of focusing his energy on beating his competitors in court, he should focus his energy on creating the most innovative product, always being one step ahead of his competitors and winning with innovation. In the end, he was thankful for being able to express his fears to someone and look at them in a critical and somewhat objective manner.

Stephen shares:

During my stepson Elliot's second year of university studies, he decided to be a franchisee for a student painting company. He believed he could make $100,000 in sales and $35,000 in profits over the summer months. After booking only about $1,000 in sales the first month, he received an invoice from the company for $6,000 in marketing materials he never even used. After reading the fine print, he learned he was obliged to take and pay for these materials. The worst-case scenario for him was that he'd lose more money than he made and do a lot of hard work for a negative return. He was a student and every dollar counted, and he began putting more and more time into his franchise. In order to maximize potential sales, he had to be organized well in advance of the summer season, when the painting could begin. He did this, compromising his studies and becoming consumed by his small company. He was driven and extremely unhappy. In reflecting on what he could do to turn around his very small business, he shared his concern with his new bride. After listening attentively, she was drawn to her husband's plight and was very motivated to help in whatever way she could. She had sales experience and offered to come with him on sales calls. They made a much more effective team together than Elliot had been alone. His sales call closing ratio went from 5 percent to 50 percent. Although he never reached the ideal reality of $100,000 in sales, at least he made a few dollars. He learned that his future was not in sales or entrepreneurship, as he didn't really enjoy managing his staff either. In fact, as a result of this experience, Elliot decided to change careers, go back to school, and become a doctor.

Expressing fears to another person is an extremely therapeutic experience—ideally, everyone should have a space where she feels comfortable talking about her fears. Sometimes we discover our worries are exaggerated, and this allows us to be free and live in the moment. Other times, we recognize that they are not, but we can come to terms with them.

One of the cruelest punishments in the world is solitary confinement. In solitary confinement, you have no one to whom you can express your fears. They drive you mad because you have no one to empathize with you and tell you that you're not alone. Having a worst-case scenario dialogue in your own head when you're alone can be a dangerous (and terrifying!) thing; this is why we encourage you to talk about your worst-case scenario with your partner, openly and honestly. Facing your fears with someone is one of the most powerful and bonding experiences you can have with another person, and is well worth the time and effort. Close friends or peer groups, either in person or even online, allow for that to happen.

Defining Your Worst-Case Scenario

When you wake up in the middle of the night, drenched in cold sweat from a nightmare about a problem you're facing, this is your worst-case scenario. It exposes your most personal fears and concerns. It's usually what both persons in a conflict are trying to avoid or prevent from happening. Sometimes you may be afraid of sharing your fears aloud; you worry that it might create a self-fulfilling prophecy, or you fear being perceived as paranoid and weak. It's critical, however, to look at these fears in broad daylight to assess how real they are for you. Bringing them to light sometimes causes them to evaporate.

Many companies analyze worst-case scenarios when they use risk-management techniques; for example, a large oil company might need to be cautious of large environmental, political, and economic changes. The oil company employs analysts to strategize and plan out how they will behave in response to various worst-case scenarios. These analysts try to answer how the company would act if there were, say, a tornado, a fire, or a terrorist attack. Similarly, militaries use war games to simulate worst-case scenarios. They act out chemical warfare and coordinated land/air attacks, among many others, to better prepare for these events.

Amir shares:

I was working with a family in which there was a conflict between the parents and their young adult child. When we began talking about the future, the child stated to her parents, "I don't really see myself as part of this family, and I don't see you having a relationship with your grandchildren." This was a huge alarm for the parents. It signaled to them that the strict way they had been acting toward their child had gone overboard and backfired on them. From then on, the parents tried to be less confrontational, deal with the true underlying conflict, and accept the child for who she really was.

As you can see, whether it calms or alarms you, imagining the worst-case scenario can benefit you when it comes to managing conflicts leading to a change of action and/or state of mind.

Key Points

- Your worst-case scenario is a personal reflection of your deepest fears.
- This is the shadow lurking behind your real underlying conflict, what you are trying to avoid or prevent from happening.
- By exposing your fears, you not only clarify your fears for yourself, but you give your partner an opportunity to understand your fears and empathize with them.
- The worst-case scenario helps mobilize you toward action or dismissing certain negative thoughts.

Exercise

Identifying Your Fears

List/identify your fears regarding the beliefs you outlined in chapter 5. Reflect how these fears may be contributing to the conflicts in your life.

Chapter 8

Step 3: Co-Create

*Your vision will become clear only when you look
into your heart.
Who looks outside, dreams. Who looks inside,
awakens.*
—Carl Jung, founder of analytical psychology

Visualization is daydreaming with a purpose.
—Bo Bennett, American businessman

Best-Case Scenario? Visualize Facts and Feelings

What do successful people like Oprah Winfrey, Arnold Schwarzenegger, and Will Smith have in common (besides living in California)? They—and many others—use visualization techniques to help achieve their goals. Visualization is when you close your eyes and try to experience your *best-case* scenario. If your best-case scenario is to have your offer accepted in a business negotiation, you imagine yourself pitching the offer with confidence. You see the positive responses on the listeners' faces, and you feel the firm handshake of final approval. You even experience the adrenaline rush of landing the deal and how both sides celebrate afterward. Over time, visualization actually trains your imagination to help facilitate what you want. The practice seeps into your subconscious mind and leads you on a focused path toward your goal. When you encounter daily choices, you will act in a way that is aligned with your visualization and toward your goals. Your intention creates an intent, which translates into focus and manifested results.

Amir and Stephen share:

> During the process of writing this book, we visualized having the finished product in our hands, books lined up in the back of the meeting room, and books available for the public at large. We had a positive image of the impact that the lessons already had in many lives, and visualizing this as being more widely available helped us push through challenges and kept us on a straight path toward completing our goal. The visualization operated as a magnet for us to channel our energy directly toward it.

Professional athletes also take advantage of visualization. A basketball player can "practice" his foul shots while sitting on the couch and imagining he is doing so. Repetition of this practice and using visualization while also performing the physical action makes the impact stronger. For example, when Jack Nicklaus and many current champions practice golf, they visualize the swing that will make the shot, the trajectory of the ball flying through the air, and where the ball will land, as well the feelings in which the successful shot will result.

Stephen shares:

> I'm an amateur tennis player who enjoys a competitive game. In order to make the fastest, most direct, and most accurate serve, I apply the visualization technique that I learned years ago from my holistic psychology coach, Dr. Stephane Bensoussan. In order to best visualize, he taught me that I would have to relax first, clear my head, and then imagine a desired outcome. I imagine where the ball will go and how quickly, in order to give myself the advantage in the game. It took a lot of discipline to do this imagining before every serve, but time and time again, the difference in the serves I was able to make with the technique versus without the technique was remarkable.
>
> First, I relax myself by closing my eyes, breathing deeply. I then imagine my serve and exactly where the ball will land. Once visualized, in a relaxed manner, I simply allow the serve to be executed through me (as in *Zen and the Art of Archery*). This takes just a few seconds and when I practice enough, it works quickly and well.

Muhammad Ali, the former world heavyweight champion, once said, "The man with no imagination has no wings." Ali would rehearse boxing matches in his head, over and over again, before the actual fight. Due to the power of visualization (and, of course, his brilliant boxing), Ali was able to win seventeen out of nineteen fights, in which he predicted the outcome exactly. Many of Ali's critics considered him to be cocky, but for his admirers, Ali's belief that he was "the greatest" was what set him apart from his competitors. Henry Ford said, "If you think you can do a thing or think you can't do a thing, you're right." Visualization is not a magic genie; rather, it helps us develop clarity on what we want, which hopefully will lead to action to make it happen.

Facts and Feelings

Visualization includes imagining the facts that you want to become real and the feelings you will feel when that happens. Here are some questions to ask yourself in preparation for visualization:

Facts
- *How do things look when all is exactly as I wish them to be?*
- *What great results have I achieved?*
- *What does my positive environment look like?*

Feelings
- *What positive emotions am I feeling in this scenario?*
- *What energy do I project when I feel this way?*
- *How am I when I feel this way?*

Your Best-Case Scenario

Your best-case scenario should be a stretch of the imagination but not a fantasy. Imagine your ideal reality by looking at yourself as if you are physically in the future that you want to create. You should figuratively attach a giant rubber band to yourself and have it pull you into that future. If your best-case scenario is too unrealistic, you will not feel a healthy tension when you try to pull. If your best-case scenario is realistic, you should feel attracted to it and energized by it. In other words, your best-case scenario should make you feel hopeful, not fearful or cynical. The imaginary rubber band represents the tension between your desire for the future and your existing starting point. The positive tension between the present and the future motivates you to act toward your best-case scenario.

Amir shares:

> A close friend of mine told me about a presentation he had coming up with the local city council. He is an architect, and he wanted to pitch a great project idea to the board. When I asked him how much money he wanted to make on the deal, he said it would be great to get $200,000 but then said, "That will never happen." I asked him how he could aim for and convince others of such a number when he himself felt it was impossible. In the end, he decided that $100,000 would be a fantastic yet not a fantasy number. Ultimately, he worked harder and with more energy to gain the $100,000 than he would have, had he aimed for $200,000. This is because he could actually see that number as a possibility, and it was something that excited and motivated him without second-guessing himself and bidding so high he would have lost the project.

There is a delicate balance between aiming too high and too low when creating your best-case scenario. Finding this balance depends on your evaluation of what's possible; fantasy to one person may seem like a rational goal to another person. If you truly believe in yourself and your potential around the issue at hand, then dream big. But if you can't imagine your grand scenario becoming true, then it's best to stay with what you can envision at this time. You can always adjust your visualization later. If you can't see it, then it can't happen, though you should always push yourself.

While you should be able to "see" your best-case scenario, it is not suggested that you create extremely low expectations to ensure that all your expectations are met, like playing volleyball and not taking the risk to spike. There should be some element of risk or uncertainty, or your goal won't inspire you, because the reward will be too small. For example, when working with a team in a company, you might volunteer for less risky tasks because you're afraid that if you aim for something more ambitious, you'll disappoint your team members, and your supervisors will evaluate you poorly. Even though you shouldn't push yourself into the world of fantasy, consider taking some risks rather than taking none at all. When you have the goal that inspires you, it both helps you to focus on the important steps you need to take to achieve it and to see problems along the way as opportunities.

Think of Martin Luther King Jr.'s "I Have a Dream" speech. When Dr. King gave this speech in 1963, it seemed like pure fantasy that a day would come when white children and black children would walk hand in hand "as sisters and brothers." Today, however, Dr. King's best-case scenario has inspired change and led us to a day where discrimination of any kind is considered unethical and often illegal. Many of Dr. King's critics thought he was crazy for imagining the scenario, but because of his vision, determination, and effort (and that of many other human rights activists and the public at large), he was able to make huge leaps toward his goal.

This brings us to the importance of not only visualizing your best-case scenario but also making an action plan to bring it into reality. Obviously, merely seeing yourself as the CEO of a multimillion dollar company or imagining yourself in a harmonious marriage is not enough for these things to come true. Visualization is the first step because it clarifies your target and gives you positive energy to keep moving forward. In the next two chapters, we'll show you how to create an action plan toward your best-case scenario.

Working Toward a Shared Vision

In visualizing your best-case scenario, see what it would look like if your personal needs and desires were fulfilled, and then share this vision with your partner. Work together to visualize a scenario that includes your ideas and your partner's ideas for a best-case scenario. You can write ideas on your worksheet or even draw images on blank paper. However you express yourselves, make sure that both you and your partner understand and are happy with the scenario you've imagined together.

To take your best-case scenario even further, imagine what would be best for the greater good (e.g., your community or the world at large). For example, if you're in conflict with your spouse, imagine how improving your marriage could create a more peaceful environment for your entire family and, as a result, even your descendants. Try to think beyond your immediate problem, and see what common values a resolution to your conflict could support. Ask yourself, *How can our best-case scenario make our family, company, or community a better place for all?* Remember, Dr. King's vision was not just about ending segregation but about creating a better society for all.

Key Points

- Your best-case scenario is a stretch of the imagination but not a fantasy.
- Use visualization techniques to experience your best-case scenario.
- Close your eyes and imagine yourself in the future, experiencing your best-case scenario.
- Ask yourself: *How do things look for me when things are exactly as they should be? What results have I achieved? What are my positive feelings?*
- Research has shown that training your imagination through visualization techniques can help focus and facilitate what you want.

Exercises

1. Creative Visualization

Get into a comfortable position, either sitting or lying down in a quiet place where you won't be disturbed, and relax your body completely. Imagine a very pleasant, safe place for you, such as an ideal country setting or maybe a beachfront. Breathe deeply, letting all tension flow out of your body. Count down slowly from ten to one, feeling yourself getting more relaxed with each count. See yourself in this place in the future, and experience the joy that comes with seeing and feeling that everything is exactly as it should be. Allow yourself to truly be surrounded by these sights, sounds, and feelings. Now that you are relaxed . . .

Set your goal. Decide on something you would like to have and work toward.

- Create a clear idea or picture of the reality that you want. Think of it in the present tense as already existing the way you want it to be. Picture yourself in the situation, and include as many details as you can.

- Focus on it often by bringing the mental picture to your mind. Focus on it closely, yet in a light, gentle way. Give it positive energy by contemplating it in a positive and encouraging way. Make strong, positive statements to yourself that it exists, that it has come or is now coming to you. Suspend any doubts or negative preconceptions you may have. If your goal changes or if its importance to you decreases, change your energy. When you achieve a goal, be sure to consciously acknowledge to yourself that it has been completed. Thank the universe for fulfilling your request.

2. Bringing Your Ideal Reality to Life

Create a collage of your best-case scenario. Gather together old magazines and cut out any images that move you and help you tap into the positive feelings and images you're aiming for in your future. Share your collage with your partner, and ask what he sees in the collage and what resonates with him. Then express to him what you chose and why. Reverse, share, and identify what you have in common, and discuss your important differences until you merge toward one shared vision. You can also accomplish this with some popular websites, such as Pinterest, which Stephen uses for inspirational images and quotations from peacemakers.

Chapter 9

Controllable Obstacles to Achieving Your Best-Case Scenario

If you can find a path with no obstacles, it probably doesn't lead anywhere.
—Frank A. Clark, politician

Your obstacles are the specific challenges that block you from reaching each element of your best-case scenario. They can range from internal obstacles, such as your mind-set or lack of knowledge, to external obstacles, like the behavior of others or your resources.

The best way to identify your obstacles is to think of the key elements of your best-case scenario, and then write down what is blocking those individual elements. Take a look at the example below:

Anne and Rick are having conflicts about money on a weekly basis, and it's starting to affect all aspects of their relationship, including trust, respect, and intimacy. Rick is more of a spender, and Anne is more of a saver.

Real, underlying conflict: There's a difference between the couple's spending personalities, which both were affected by how their parents dealt with money at their homes when Anne and Rick were growing up. Anne's father was also a spender, and it led to the family having to move every year to less and less desirable neighborhoods. Anne had to change schools almost each time and had few friends as a result. She associates overspending with the suffering of her childhood.

Rick came from a wealthy household. Both of his parents worked very long hours, travelled constantly, and compensated for their lack of attention to Rick by giving him everything he wanted in terms of toys, clothes, and gadgets. He never had to work for what he received or do chores around the house for his high allowance. For him, money represented affection, which was how his parents showed it to him in their absence.

In reviewing the Nonflict way, Anne and Rick discussed their **facts and feelings** about money and realized they were products of their past on this sensitive issue. They understood that when Anne got upset with Rick's buying another gadget, it was because to her, it triggered the pain and fear of losing their home. For Rick, spending without restriction made him feel loved, and cutting that off meant she didn't really love him. For both of them, money clearly represented more than just money.

In relation to the conflict over money, they openly discussed **what was working well for them** and the state of their finances, and they realized they had a very healthy balance sheet together; both of them had secure jobs with substantial incomes. They also loved each other and wanted to have children soon. They were a good complementary team that balanced each other.

Their **worst-case scenario,** if this conflict wasn't resolved, was that they'd continue to fight, grow farther apart, and potentially eventually divorce. They had learned that unresolved money conflicts were one of the leading causes for divorce, something they clearly wanted to avoid.

They came up with their **best-case scenario**—that they both trust each other's good judgment, feel loved independent of money, and they have enough money to feel secure, have children, and eventually retire in comfort.

Obstacles

- Anne and Rick haven't discussed how much money is enough to meet their needs and desires.
- Having a child would mean Anne's not working for a period of time, and that would impact their income. If they have other children, it would mean more time off work and more child-related expenses.
- If they have more than one child, it likely will mean they will need to move to a larger home, requiring more money.
- Anne and Rick have to agree on what a comfortable retirement means; at what age, how much money would have to be saved, and when to start doing so.
- Anne's and Rick's parents are retired now, and if they needed financial help from Anne and Rick, it might get in the way of their plans.

Breaking up the obstacles into small, digestible parts makes resolving the conflict more manageable. By examining one obstacle at a time together, the conflict seemed less overwhelming.

Key Points

- Obstacles are specific challenges that block you from reaching your best-case scenario.
- Breaking up the real conflict into smaller units makes resolving the conflict much easier.

Exercise

Identifying Your Own Money Attitudes

What are your own beliefs about money? If money is an issue causing conflict in your life, various online tools may help in understanding its cause, such as the Money Motto at http://veritage.ca/moneymotto.

 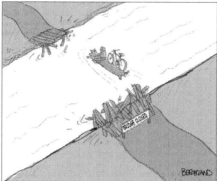

Chapter 10

Overcoming Controllable Obstacles

*God, grant me the serenity to accept the things I
cannot change,
the courage to change the things I can, and the
wisdom to know the difference.*
—Reinhold Niebuhr, "Serenity Prayer"

*There are two ways of meeting difficulties:
You alter the difficulties or you alter yourself
meeting them.*
—Phyllis Bottome, British novelist

Controllable vs. Uncontrollable Obstacles

Now that you have identified the obstacles to your best-case
scenario, you must divide them into obstacles that you can
control or influence and obstacles that you can't. There's no

use in spending time and effort on obstacles that are fixed and unchangeable or out of your range of possible influence. It's best to simply accept them as facts of life and move on. This is, in fact, the essence of ancient Stoic philosophy—one of the leading philosophical schools among the ancient Greeks and Romans. Here are some examples of uncontrollable obstacles:

- The feelings and behaviors of others. You can influence others' feelings and behaviors but only if they allow you. Ultimately, the choice to change is theirs.
- Forces that you deem more powerful than yourself. Some examples, using Rick and Anne's situation, would be the existence of inflation, the rate of return on the stock or bond market as a whole, and the laws on government pension benefits affecting them and their parents.

Learning to accept things outside your control frees you to focus on the things you can control. While you can't control how others feel or behave, you can control how you react to or view these things.

Creating an Action Plan

Once you know which obstacles you can affect, you can brainstorm together on the steps to take that will help to overcome these obstacles. Decide on who will do these tasks, what the tasks entail, and when each task will be completed. The more specific and measurable the tasks are, the more likely it is that they'll be accomplished. Try to create a work plan for three to six months into the future that will excite both you and your partner. Start with baby steps and grow from there.

If you can't decide which steps to take to tackle the controllable obstacles, look at the exercises at the end of this chapter for brainstorming ideas.

For Rick and Anne, deciding on how much money they need to meet their desires requires that they work together on a budget. Getting their situation on paper helps them both understand it better and allows for constructive decision-making. Their expenses may include some room for discretionary spending so that Rick doesn't feel totally stifled and resentful, yet meeting Anne's need for security. Their budget could then include "what if" scenarios in terms of Anne leaving her job, having one or more children, and moving into another house. They'd also want to talk to their parents to see how likely it is that they will need financial or other support from Rick and Anne. By co-creating their ideal reality, the couple actually can become closer than ever, with a greater level of trust and mutual respect.

Ensuring Accountability and Follow-Up

Asking and answering the questions of "who will do what, when?" ensures accountability and brings closure to the conversation. Afterward, all parties and perspectives should feel satisfied that the issue is being taken care of and that this process was not merely an exercise in dialogue but something that led to tangible results. Sometimes it's enough to share how each side views the conflict and feels, but most of the time we need to ensure that people will follow through and act. It's important, therefore, to create mechanisms that ensure mutual accountability. As part of your action plan, decide on a date when you'll meet for a follow-up. If you're in a workplace, you can write down your action plan and post in on the wall in your office or use your productivity software. If you're at home, you can post your action plan on the fridge (or soon use your fridge's productivity software). Encourage and support each other to follow the action plan so you can live out your co-created future.

Resolving the conflict together also leaves the door open for more constructive continued communication. As circumstances change, the solution can be improved, amended, and changed.

Anne and Rick decided that she would keep the books for the both of them, which gave her great comfort. Rick has his monthly allowance, which includes some discretionary money that he can either spend or save for a new gadget coming out later in the year. They both understood and agreed they wanted a child within three years, so they have to put money aside for that, now part of their budget. They also changed their vacation plans, realizing they would be almost as happy going by car to a beautiful lake town four hours away as to an island resort, which would have cost $5,000 more. They also agreed to review their finances together every three months to ensure they are meeting their objectives.

Key Points

- First, divide the obstacles into obstacles that you can influence and obstacles that are out of your control. Focus on what you can control, and accept the obstacles that you cannot control.
- Next, delegate tasks to practically overcome controllable obstacles. Ask who will do these tasks, and decide what the tasks entail and when each task will be completed.
- Make a long-term plan.
- Ensure accountability and closure to the conversation.

Exercises

1. Round-Robin Brainstorming

If you're using the Nonflict way with a partner and you cannot come up with a resolution to your conflict, consider bringing the obstacle(s) to a group setting, such as your family or to your company's or organization's board. Explain the Nonflict way and obstacle(s) to the group and the full set of potential consequences. Then ask everyone to write down ideas for solutions on a piece of paper, and ask each person to share his ideas and write them on a whiteboard in front of the group. Note if there are repeats, and make checkmarks next to those ideas. It is important that each person take her own time to brainstorm before anyone presents to the group, as sometimes when one person shares an idea, the rest get excited by that idea and forget what their original ideas were. This technique maximizes the diversity of ideas from which to choose.

Another technique is to have each person share his written ideas on paper with the person on his right, who then can add variations of the first person's ideas underneath each of them. Each person then shares her own and her partner's ideas with the group.

2. "If I Were . . ."

In order to shift your perspective, imagine if you were someone else facing this same obstacle. If you were your best friend, your mother, or a famous expert in the area of the conflict, how would you resolve this conflict? Let your mind wander and really delve into the person's personality and behaviors.

3. Change Makers

If you are still having difficulty coming up with potential solutions, first go back and make sure there is "nothing else" to discuss concerning facts and feelings. Take a moment to review the process to this point. Have you forgotten anything? If you have not resolved the issue yet, it doesn't mean the issue is unresolvable, so don't be discouraged. Sometimes problems take longer to resolve. Sometimes it is a question of outside factors that need to align. What is important is that all the parties are interested in resolution and have the patience and tenacity to work on it until it evolves. If you are still discouraged, make a list of two or three individuals whom you respect very much who have changed the course of history (e.g., Martin Luther King Jr., Gandhi). Then imagine how our world would be different today if these individuals had felt that they couldn't achieve their goals. Then you can agree to a time and date to return to the problem to work on coming up with a resolution plan again.

Chapter 11

The Nonflict Way in Different Settings

That which is hateful to you, do not do to your fellow. That is the whole Torah; the rest is the explanation.
—Rabbi Hillel, first-century Jewish scholar

I can start by talking about our differences, and I may never get to our commonalities, or I can start by talking about what we have in common amongst our religions and . . . maybe—just maybe—the differences would take care of themselves.
—Imam Dr. Zijad Delic, religious leader

To this point, we've talked about how to use the Nonflict way in basic two-person conflicts. Now we will explain how it can be applied to other kinds of conflicts, such as internal conflicts, group conflicts, and global conflicts—which may be based on identity.

Internal Conflicts

Internal conflicts are conflicts we have inside our own minds over conflicting interests, desires, and ideas. At some point in our lives, we all face internal conflicts over the work/family balance, the freedom/responsibility balance, and more. Part of being human is having a complex assortment of thoughts that sometimes contradict each other. One very common internal conflict is over food. The competing desires of eating all kinds of rich choices that tease us and avoiding the urge to overeat and making healthier choices can be frustrating and chronic. There is so much stimulation around us, from billboards and television to smells and tempting foods laid out. Choosing the foods that we know will help us maintain or reach a healthy state can be very difficult.

Amir shares his story (to which Stephen relates as well):

> I have been struggling with the internal conflict over my weight and eating habits for years. I have read many articles describing how to lose weight, and I have scanned more than just a few books about dieting. As I practiced sports intensively, I also had some experience with self-discipline. I knew, for instance, that even though I initially would feel extremely optimistic about the task I had taken upon myself to complete, I would have to be careful not to become overconfident. I say this because at the beginning of a new diet, I always felt powerful, but after a few days, my mind would start to rationalize my poor choices. I would tell myself, "I've been so good; I deserve this piece of cake," or instead of eating a chocolate chip muffin, I would

eat three chocolate chip granola bars because "that's healthy." Everything slowly went downhill, because I was too good at finding the loopholes in my own rules.

Sometimes I woke up in the middle of the night, full of unnecessary calories from a big dinner with sugar and fat—and the regret that accompanied it. I would start planning how I was going to take things more seriously the next day. But then I would remember that I would be traveling all day to business meetings. Business meetings usually meant eating carbs and more carbs. If the company I was working with was "health conscious," they might put out a couple of two-week-old apples, but most of the food offered was high in carbohydrates. You know how this story ends: On a good day, I would only eat a chocolate croissant and stash an apple away in my bag for later. That counted for something, right?

If you'd like to use Nonflict to solve an internal conflict, use the same steps as you would for an external conflict. To do this, first separate your conflicting desires as if they were the desires of two separate people. Sometimes we see this depicted in cartoons as an angel sitting on one shoulder and a devil sitting on the other. More often than not, the desires will not be diametrically opposed, but they may simply represent slightly different versions of us.

For example, if you're experiencing an internal conflict about whether to start a diet or to eat whatever you want, you'd divide the desire to be healthy from the desire for freedom to eat whatever you want, and see them as represented by two separate people. Think of your internal conflict as an actual conflict between a health-focused person and a freedom-focused person. As you go through the steps of the Nonflict way, whenever you read the words "you" and "your partner," replace them with the representations of the two desires in your mind. (We don't expect you to mirror yourself, but make sure that you're clear on the facts and feelings of both desires.) When you get to Step 3: Co-Create, imagine having both of these people sit down and work to satisfy both of their desires.

For example:

Step 1: Understand Yourself and Your Partner

Health-focused person:

The conflict is that I'm constantly tempted to break my diet when I see foods that look good and are tasty, which happen to have high calorie and fat content. This makes me feel like I lack self-control, and I can't stick to a disciplined routine, which frustrates me and lowers my self-esteem. It's important for me to make smart choices when it comes to food because it affects my overall health and how much energy and vitality I have in my everyday life.

Freedom-focused person:

The conflict is that I feel limited by these diets that restrict me and make me feel imprisoned. I have so many other things I have to control in my life. Why can't I just enjoy myself when it comes to food? When I'm sticking to a diet, I feel like I'm missing out on a part of life that I deserve to enjoy because I work so hard in other things. Dieting makes me feel stressed and worried. It's important for me to feel relaxed when I'm not working or enjoying free time with my family.

Step 2: Understand Your Shared Reality

The real, underlying conflict:

Competing desires. A conflict between wanting to be healthy and wanting to feel free and relaxed—letting go, living the moment, enjoying being careless and spontaneous.

What's working well?

I realize I have a problem. I've made other huge steps toward improving my health, like regularly exercising. I have friends and family who will support me in this struggle. I know what is good for me.

Worst-case scenario:

Either I will continue to eat whatever I like and gain a lot of weight—which will impact my self-esteem, my ability to keep up with the kids, and my overall health—or I will continue to diet and feel constrained, like I'm not living life to its full potential.

Step 3: Co-Create

Ideal reality:

I feel healthy and happy. I have the energy and strength to participate in all kinds of physical activities, including sports, dance, and being wild with my kids. I am able to enjoy my favorite foods and eat out with friends. I feel excited about traveling and no longer worry about how I'm going to eat well during business trips. My mind is clear and at peace. I've found a solution that works for the long-term.

Obstacles to achieving my best-case scenario:

- *The nature of my job, which requires me to travel constantly, which creates uncertainty about which foods are available and makes eating healthily more difficult*
- *The stress I feel, which pushes me over the edge, weakens my self-control, and encourages me to eat sweets*
- *The lack of time to prepare healthy options at home or just being plain lazy*

- *My inability to commit to a diet, which may relate to a lack of belief in myself*
- *The fact that many healthy foods do not seem to satisfy my urges*

What can I do to overcome controllable obstacles?

- *I do not want to change the nature of my job, because I love what I do and the impact I make on people's lives, but I can pack some healthier options to take with me in case the companies I visit don't have healthy options available for lunch and snacks.*
- *I can control my stress levels by taking ten minutes every morning to meditate or by doing various types of exercise.*
- *I can control my time at home better, either by preparing a large amount of food at the beginning of the week, which I can eat as needed throughout the week, or by asking my family to help me prepare these foods.*
- *I can impact my attitude by spending time reflecting on how I've overcome obstacles in the past. I can apply what I learned on committing to a plan when the end result was really important.*
- *I can choose role models in friends who have the right eating patterns.*
- *I cannot control how certain foods taste, but I can meet with a dietician who can teach me about healthy foods that would be more appealing.*
- *I can change my self-perception about who is in control here and what is truly best for me.*

Through following Nonflict, Amir's weight and health is happily moving in the right direction.

Within Groups

We realize that not all external conflicts occur between two people. In our families, in our organizations, and in our communities, conflicts can involve many different individuals. This doesn't mean that Nonflict gets more complicated; it stays the same. The key modification is to assign a leader. If more than two people are involved in a conflict, the process will take more time. You need to listen to all the perspectives involved, but if each person mirrored each perspective, it would be exhausting and frustrating. We suggest instead that you assign one person in the group—someone who is familiar with the process—to lead each person through Step 1 and to mirror these perspectives for the entire group. This leader will ensure that the group stays on target and maintains momentum. She will also be crucial in synthesizing these perspectives and helping the group find their real, underlying conflict in Step 2 and a resolution that respects all the interests involved in creating the group's ideal reality, Step 3.

Other Suggestions

1. **Take advantage of an audience.** Whether you have an internal conflict, a two-person conflict, or a group conflict,

use any communities that you have at your disposal as sounding boards. These can be forums in your workplace, online forums, family meetings, or meetings with your clergy. Walk the group through the conflict by going through the steps of the Nonflict way. Use the group to help you resolve complicated issues or just to get feedback on resolutions you've already found. Accept that sometimes you just can't do it all on your own, and group feedback can often point you in directions that you never saw.

2. **Take advantage of technology.** Although face-to-face conflict resolution is always the preferred method, with the advent of the global village, understanding and resolving via voice-with-video technology that allows for eye contact is better than voice alone, all of which are preferable to trying to resolve conflict by e-mail. There are more and more programs available for multi-user video conferencing technology. Stephen and Amir use Skype and Zoom.

3. **Build further group cohesion.** For further ideas on building group cohesion in families or organizations, please see the section in the appendix.

Between Groups

Amir and Stephen both have deep, personal interests in helping groups of people with historically turbulent histories learn to coexist. A large portion of our work is devoted to bringing groups in conflict together to learn how to gain mutual trust and respect.

Amir facilitates peace forums for business executives from conflict regions (such as between Israeli and Arab executives, or Greek and Turkish executives). In these transformative meetings, the group is able to break down long-standing stereotypes by learning to understand one another through listening openly and imagining how they would feel in the other's shoes.

The strict rules of confidentiality foster intimacy, which allows the members to speak in ways that reveal information that is normally unheard and filtered in the public discourse and in the media. The group members work together to define the real underlying problem by writing down their own perspectives on the conflict and synthesizing their thoughts into a commonly agreed upon conflict. They then develop a shared vision for the future and brainstorm ways to work toward this future. Nonflict's steps and questions frame all of their discussions and lead them in a constructive direction. (For more on this topic, see the addendum.)

An Israeli member shares:

> The meetings with the other side were the most meaningful things I did in my life. It was more meaningful for me than all the companies I've created and more than all the people I've employed and our prior accomplishments. Everyone on both sides came to listen and hear things that they couldn't hear from the media or their own political leadership. If you had asked me to predict the perspectives of the other side before meeting them, I would have been incorrect. Even though I'm politically involved, and I watch the news regularly, at the end of the day, these opinions are from journalists, politicians, local leaders—people who have their own agendas. But when I spoke with everyday people, I was able to understand things that I didn't understand before. I understand the priorities of the other side for the first time, what they were willing to sacrifice or not. We have a stereotype in Israel that Arabs don't want to end the conflict, but nowadays, I don't believe that.

An Arab member shares:

> From total distrust, anxiety, and perhaps even
> resentment between the two sides, we built a new
> and strong foundation of friendship and teamwork
> toward better understanding and a common future.

Stephen has used the Nonflict way to reach conflict groups
through organizing Art of Peace events that deal with the
Israeli-Palestinian conflict and the French-English conflict in
Canada. These events have taught key business and community
leaders the power of the Nonflict way and how it can transform
future negotiations. In addition to these events, Stephen also
takes the Nonflict way with him on trips around the world and
tries to take advantage of meetings in conflict zones to spread
its message. For example, it had an important impact on a trip
Stephen took in 2013 to a Palestinian refugee camp in the West
Bank.

Stephen shares:

> In the refugee camp, I visited a women's co-op
> to learn about their daily life challenges. During
> the exchange, I shared the Nonflict way with the
> women as a process for conflict resolution. After
> four hours, the meeting went from initial suspi-
> cion about Canadians to warmth and trust. The
> Palestinian women were thrilled and said they
> could use the Nonflict way with their husbands.
> They also expressed willingness to meet with Israeli
> women to see if the Nonflict way could facilitate a
> constructive dialogue and an interest in together
> cornering the politicians in a room to learn the

way and these mothers not letting them leave until there was an agreement for peace. This experience showed me the power of the Nonflict way and how it can inspire people to take risks. For these women, meeting with Israelis could lead to severe negative consequences (they could be accused of being collaborators or encouraging normalization), but the Nonflict way was solid enough to make them feel safe and confident that taking that risk was worth the reward. The experience of these women who were willing to take the risk also inspired me to use the Nonflict way for my own internal conflict—on what should I focus my future? The process led me to take the risk of leaving a secure career in real estate to focus on sharing the Nonflict way full time.

Key Points

- With minor adjustment, the Nonflict way works for internal conflicts and those within and between groups as well.
- For internal conflict, separate your conflicting desires as if they were the desires of two separate people, and go through the steps.
- For conflicts within a group, assign a moderator to lead the process and mirror the members where required.
- For conflicts between groups, an impartial facilitator could be used to take the parties though the Nonflict way. If none is available, members of each group ideally would become familiar with the Nonflict way and work together through the process to resolution.

Exercise

Identifying Your Own Internal Conflicts

We all have internal conflicts. Reflect on one that you are facing, and go through the Nonflict way to help resolve it.

Chapter 12

Preparation for Nonflict Discussions

Before anything else, preparation is the key to
success.
—Alexander Graham Bell

P roper preparation before engaging in a constructive
conflict-resolution session is critical to its success. Acting
out or reacting with your first impulse while surrounded
by others usually doesn't lead to the most effective results.

1. **Find a quiet place.** Choose an environment where you will
   not be interrupted.
2. **Sit facing your partner.**
3. **Refer to the Nonflict way or worksheet in the appendix.**
   Explain the Nonflict way to your partner.
4. **Check for consent.** Make sure that both parties are completely willing to engage in a conflict-resolution process using the Nonflict way.

What If My Partner Doesn't Consent To Using The Nonflict Way?

Your partner may not want to try something new or may suspect that you're trying to manipulate the situation in your favor by using the Nonflict way. The only way to overcome this hurdle is to create an atmosphere in which your partner feels respected and sees that you're trying to understand her. This might involve giving your partner time and space to have the conversation when she is ready. If you just had a heated fight, allowing for time and space is usually the best course of action.

When the time is right, start the conversation by asking your partner the questions in the Nonflict way (the three steps shown in Chapter 2), and practice active listening and mirroring (see Chapter 4) *without asking your partner to do the same for you.* Most people naturally will feel more comfortable when they are listened to first. If you can mirror your partner's comments with a calm tone, demonstrating empathy and providing your partner with validation, this can transform your partner's mental state into one that is more willing to hear your side of the story.

What If My Partner Still Refuses To Listen To Me?

If your partner is still not ready to engage with you, you may want to find an impartial third party to lead you through the Nonflict way. This third party would act as a facilitator, making sure both people in the conflict stay on track by answering the right questions and mirroring at the appropriate times. If the partners are really upset with each other and refuse to mirror one another, the facilitator can serve as the mirror of each person. The third party would not speak about his feelings or interrupt the other people but would ensure that both parties follow the process in the Nonflict way. Good examples of facilitators are therapists who have read this book (to facilitate between spouses), parents (to facilitate between siblings), or a mutually respected and trusted colleague at work who is willing to read this book and help. After getting help in using the process, the parties should be able to resolve future conflicts themselves using the Nonflict way.

Whichever path you take to initiate the conversation, find a way that both parties are comfortable with. Neither party should feel backed into a corner. When people feel trapped, they do not open up. This point is crucial in ensuring a respectful and effective process.

Once you're both on the same page, take your time in moving through the three steps.

Remember to:
- breathe deeply by inhaling and exhaling, long and slow; and
- keep calm eye contact by focusing gently without staring.

Chapter 13

The Nonflict Way:
A Brief Overview

You may have had one major conflict in mind when you started this book and then realized how the Nonflict way could be used for several other conflicts, including internal ones. As with any new skill, the more you practice it, the better you'll get. Soon, you may want to share your life lessons and experiences with others.

Stephen and Amir have started a nonprofit organization called Million Peacemakers to spread the use of these tools to families, businesses, and communities. Please visit us at www.millionpeacemakers.org, where we will post useful information and new insights and experiences, and where you can also find useful tools. We invite you to be one in a million too!

Here is an overview with key take-aways from each of the steps of the Nonflict way:

Step 1: Understand Yourself and Your Partner

A. Share your view of the conflict: *What is the conflict? How does it make me feel?*

What is important to me?

- An individual's personal framing determines how he views a particular situation or conflict.
- By recognizing the existence of framing, we are better equipped to communicate because we are encouraged to accept the viewpoints of others as equivalent to our own (versus "right" or "wrong"). This leads to a resolution that takes into account all relevant perspectives.
- Constructive communication uses simple "I" statements without blaming or shaming your partner.
- Self-awareness and the ability to be honest and vulnerable with your partner are all key elements in ensuring that your needs in any discussion are met.

B. Your partner mirrors the essence of what you have said and asks, *Have I understood you well? Is there anything else?*
- Mirroring depends on active listening. Pay attention to your partner's words, emotions, body language, and tone.
- Mirroring means paraphrasing, not repeating word for word.
- Mirroring requires empathy. Put your ego aside, and step into the shoes of your partner.
- As humans, we have a large capacity to empathize with others, no matter how angry they may be.
- Mirroring lends to validation. Validation builds trust and helps your partner to open up to you.
- After your partner mirrors you, switch roles and repeat.
- Asking "Is there anything else?" encourages you and your partner to dig deeper into the real underlying cause of the conflict.

Step 2: Understand Your Shared Reality

A. You and your partner discuss together, asking yourselves, *What is our real underlying conflict?*

- Distinguish between causes and symptoms. The cause is the source of the "real conflict."
- Don't get bogged down in specific actions or people.
- Focus on the total, all-encompassing issue.
- Ask yourselves, why are these two, equally valid perspectives clashing?

B. *What is working well for us?*
- "What is working well for us" means "What is working well for our relationship, and what do I appreciate about the other person?"
- Maybe the only thing that's working well is that both parties want to resolve the conflict; you can still recognize this.
- Research has shown that positive discussions yield positive results.

C. *What is our worst-case scenario?* Visualize facts and feelings.
- Your worst-case scenario is a personal reflection of your deepest fears.
- This is the shadow lurking behind your real conflict. It is what you are trying to avoid or prevent from happening.
- By exposing your fears, you not only clarify your fears for yourself, but you give your partner an opportunity to understand your fears and empathize with them.
- Both parties often imagine the same worst-case scenario if they each break it down to its most basic elements.
- Discussing the worst-case scenario becoming a reality motivates us to find a solution.

Step 3: Co-Create

A. You and your partner discuss together, *What is our best-case scenario?* Visualize facts and feelings.

- Your best-case scenario is a stretch of the imagination. It's your ideal reality. Think outside the box.
- Use visualization techniques to experience your best-case scenario.
- Ask yourself, what am I doing? How am I feeling? What does my environment look and feel like?
- Research has shown that training your imagination through visualization techniques can help facilitate what you want.

B. *What are the obstacles to achieving our best-case scenario?*
- Obstacles are specific challenges that block you from reaching your best-case scenario.
- These are the smaller units that comprise your real conflict.
- Breaking up the real conflict into smaller units makes resolving the conflict much easier.

C. *What can we do to overcome controllable obstacles? Who will do what, when?*
- First, divide the obstacles into obstacles that you can influence and obstacles that are out of your control. Focus on ones you can control and influence.
- Next, delegate tasks. Ask, who will do these tasks? What do the tasks entail? When will each task be completed?
- Break the tasks into small steps so that neither party gets overwhelmed.
- Make a long-term plan.
- This step ensures accountability and closure to the conversation.

The Nonflict Way

Step 1: Understand Yourself and Your Partner

Share your view of the conflict.

What is the conflict? How does it make me feel? What is important for me?

Your partner mirrors the essence of what you have said and asks,

Did I understand you well? Is there anything else?

(*You and your partner switch roles and repeat the questions above.*)

Step 2: Understand Your Shared Reality

You and your partner discuss together, asking yourselves:

What is our real underlying conflict?

What is working well for us?

What is our worst-case scenario? (Visualize facts and feelings.)

Step 3: Co-Create

You and your partner discuss together.

What is our best-case scenario? (Visualize facts and feelings.)

What are the obstacles to achieving our best-case scenario?

What can we do to overcome controllable obstacles? Who will do what, when?

The Nonflict Way
Worksheet

Your name: _____

Your partner's name: _____

Step 1: Understand Yourself and Your Partner

Before you start . . .

Reflect and write about your view of the conflict.

1. What is the conflict? How does it make you feel?

_____

_____

_____

_____

_____

_____

_____

_____

_____

_____

_____

_____

_____

_____

What is important for you?

_____

_____

_____

_____

_____

_____

_____

_____

_____

_____

_____

_____

_____

_____

Share your view of the conflict with your partner.
2. Your partner listens and mirrors the essence of what you have said.

3. Then your partner asks, *"Did I understand you well? Is there anything else?"*

(You and your partner switch roles and repeat the questions above)

While your partner is sharing his/her view . . .
Take notes in order to capture the essence of what your partner is saying. Focus on key ideas and emotions; don't record word for word. Don't lose eye contact.

_____

_____

_____

_____

_____

_____

_____

_____

_____

_____

_____

_____

Mirror the essence back to your partner.

Step 2: Understand Your Shared Reality

Reflect on and record your answers to the following questions. Then discuss your answers with your partner.

What's our real underlying conflict?

_____

_____

_____

_____

_____

_____

_____

_____

_____

What's working well for us?

_____

_____

_____

_____

_____

_____

_____

_____

What's our worst-case scenario?

Facts

_____

_____

_____

_____

_____

_____

_____

_____

_____

Feelings

_____

_____

_____

_____

_____

_____

_____

_____

_____

Step 3: Co-Create

You and your partner answer the following questions together and record your conclusions for future reference.

What's our best-case scenario?

Facts

_____

_____

_____

_____

_____

_____

_____

_____

_____

Feelings

_____

_____

_____

_____

_____

_____

_____

_____

What are the obstacles to our best-case scenario?

Controllable?		Controllable?	
_____ Yes No		_____ Yes No	
_____ Yes No		_____ Yes No	
_____ Yes No		_____ Yes No	

Action Plan for Controllable Obstacles

You

What: By when (date):

_____

_____

_____

_____

Your partner

What: By when (date):

_____

_____

_____

Addendum

Use of the Nonflict Way in Driving Social Change

We have witnessed the incredible power of the Nonflict way in effective conflict resolution. Introducing pre-emptive use of the Nonflict way through structured, continuous meetings allows issues to be dealt with before they become explosive. People in a dialogue communicate at a high level of harmony and empathy. With this kind of momentum, we can see the enormous potential to create impact at a greater scale for society as a whole. The big question is how to go about leveraging this powerful tool. We would like to share some stories with you of where this large-scale transformation already is happening

The first story takes place in India. The state of Maharashtra has 120 million inhabitants, mostly concentrated around Mumbai. Abhijit Pawar, the chairman of Sakal Media Group, leads a large media group. His principles also dictate social responsibility above and beyond simple charity. He envisioned, created, and sponsored an organization to empower women, called Tanishka (www.tanishkaforum.com). His dream was to create a catalyst for this grassroots movement that would ignite and spread social change.

This organization first identified small groups of women, usually based on where they lived. In some cases, these would be women from large apartment-building complexes, where thousands of neighbors lived. Divided into groups of twenty members each, they were encouraged to meet on a regular basis, once a month, in the center of their neighborhood. In other cases, women within a village area, who already had made informal groups, were supported in fostering a collaboration of women to run microbusinesses.

Amir was invited to train the Sakal executive team on how to run such forums for delivering change. The objective was to establish a methodology that would work in the setting of social transformation and have a positive impact on societal issues around those women, as well as dealing with the women's personal issues.

Today, these groups already number 100,000 women across the state of Maharashtra, and they have touched millions with their changes.

The Tanishka groups meet once a month. In their meetings, each and every participant identifies what works well and gives positive energy, as well as sharing what hurts or keeps her awake at night in both her personal life and her community. After all present this update, the group together decides which issue to tackle. They then develop an action plan of what to do. In following the Nonflict way:

They first analyze what the real problem is, including identifying the underlying issues and causes.

They then ask themselves what some of the things are that work well around this issue and should be appreciated or can be leveraged.

In that light, what might be the worst-case scenario?

What is the visualized ideal reality?

They look for the obstacles to achieving the ideal reality—those obstacles they can control and put into a detailed plan of action on how to overcome them, and who will do what and when.

The group might also decide to deal with personal issues, identifying challenges in their lives and in the lives of their families. They also look at other critical matters that they find in the world around them that have an impact on their lives. We have heard that they have covered large and other far-reaching social-community problems—topics such as pollution, crime and violence, domestic violence, safety for their daughters, work opportunities for women, issues with water, the health system, and the quality and accessibility of the education system for their kids and themselves.

In one village, the women created a machine to bake a typical but very labor-intensive Indian bread. Their idea was to manufacture, sell, and distribute the bread to all the surrounding villages. They formed an organization and infrastructure for the production, administration, sale, and delivery of the bread, and in so doing, they created employment and secured income for a large group of families.

One of the groups was very concerned about pollution. In their controllable ideal reality, they felt they could do something that would be inexpensive, simple, and practical. Each family planted a tree in front of their house. This clean-air–friendly act empowered them and was a symbolic message to the politicians that they were serious about their issue, motivating the local government to make positive changes as well.

In the city of Pune, the group also decided to tackle the issue of pollution but in this case in conjunction with promoting public transportation. They chose one day and marked it on the calendar, calling it a No-Car Day. They then went about promoting it, getting necessary permits, roadblocks, and the necessary support from the community at large. This city with a population of over three million successfully used only their own public transportation system on their No-Car Day. With their determination, resourcefulness, and communication skills, they managed to bring this issue to the forefront of public attention.

In some parts of India, there is a strong preference for giving birth to boys. Culturally, many families rationalize that boys, who grow into working men, tend to remain with their family and take care on the family's financial responsibility. Girls, on the other hand, are primarily expected to be homemakers. The custom is for the bride's family to provide a dowry to the groom's family, and the bride is to move in with the groom and his family after marriage. In this tradition, her family loses her as a potential income provider and as a support for her aging parents. In one particular village, the group's attention was drawn to one of their members who had given birth to a third daughter. The husband refused to have that daughter brought into his home.

News traveled very quickly, and the women felt their intervention was the only thing that would save the situation. They understood that words and verbal communication would not be enough to convince this father to change his mind. The group organized a schedule and made sure that some of them would accompany the mother at all times. They assisted her; they provided meals, took care of her, and helped with the baby, and throughout the period, they encouraged the father with kindness and love. Slowly, over the course of the next weeks, he began to fall in love with his daughter and his resistance melted away. By the time the supporting women relaxed their vigil, they left a unified new family, filled with appreciation and respect for what the group had done for them. Not only is the Tanishka movement using its collective power in dealing with their members' issues, but they also have learned that they are capable of leveraging the power they have as a group. They have close ties to their regional representation within their voting districts. They understand that, if needed, they can use media coverage and social media in order to impact politicians, law enforcement, or government to make change.

Impact can be very difficult to measure, but using the first regional election since the inception of Tanishka, there is documented proof of an impressive increase in the percentage of women who are voting. The previous average of 50 percent grew to 65 percent.

Fueled by the momentum of the groups of women, the Sakal Group realized the instant applicability this concept could have with the student population of India. There are thousands of universities and colleges across the nation. Students traditionally have a desire to come together to create networks, not only to build relationships but also to make an impact in society overall. We know that young people often are the driving force of change and are willing to be vocal and committed to their convictions, regardless of the risks, in order to make their world a better place.

Once again, Abhijit Pawar spearheaded a new initiative with the group called Young Inspirators. His company funded and facilitated the creation of steering committees at each university to act as home base, to enable the forming of groups of twenty students. Their purpose is to meet together on campus and function in much the same way as the women's groups. They share all their concerns; whether personal or university- or community-based. They deal with women's safety at night around campus, late-night traveling home, or sources for graduate employment opportunities. In the true collaborative style of the Nonflict way, projects are posted to their group website, yinforchange.org, to increase their reach. The potential for this venue is growing exponentially. As news spreads, more and more people are joining in daily, becoming a part of this transformation. There are 1,600 universities and colleges signed on in the state of Maharashtra, Sakal's home base. In the opening training in August 2014, which Amir facilitated, over 500 group leaders were trained. The goal is to now train a leader from each of the 1,600 schools, who would bring it to their universities and colleges, representing over one million students.

Our next story takes place deep in the heart of Mexico City. TV Azteca, part of the Grupo Salinas empire, is led by its president, Ricardo Salinas Pliego, who always saw the importance of using television to share information and be a good corporate citizen—a catalyst for national change. Amir has worked with the group for over twenty-two years and has worked with Elisa Salinas, leader of the Novellas production part of the business. She and the organization are committed to making an impact in the lives of women in Mexico and have created women's groups to effect the change. The first few groups were so successful that Elisa Salinas was inspired to devote network resources to a brand new TV show to promote the idea. Public awareness was created through the use of this type of television series, called a *telenovela*, a cross between a soap opera and reality TV. The dramas are portrayed by professional actors who enact the true stories of these women's groups, their conflicts successfully resolved, and the transformation they are making in society.

As in India, one idea led to another initiative—Elisa Salinas's passion, Muay Thai boxing, led to a new initiative. Recruiting a core group of instructors under the "Sport is Your Gang" banner, we trained these motivated young teachers in the Nonflict way. These thirty instructors designed a course that connected the communication skills of the Nonflict way with the sport, resulting in an experiential, tool-building, and fun environment for ten- to fifteen-year-olds. The kids from troubled backgrounds come together for the physical training and then sit together to talk about the issues in their lives, using the way of communication we have developed for them. They have become a deep, trusting support group that takes care of each other like a family.

This is only the beginning of a deep understanding of what happens when a group comes together to deal with conflicting issues, either with themselves or their community, and uses each other as sounding boards and as support groups.

The Nonflict Way in Business—Nonflict Forum

The Nonflict way's ability to transform businesses and their organizational cultures should come as no surprise. People within a given function or department have a tendency to focus on their own agendas, goals and priorities, sometimes acting at the expense of others.

It is not uncommon to adopt an "us versus them" attitude in these situations. Many organizations have experienced the consequences which can be debilitating: departments holding onto key data instead of sharing it, becoming resistant to ideas originating from outside their department, or refusing to participate in activities they are not officially responsible for.

As leaders, we have a duty to create a process where our team can properly deal with this destructive conflict, but also an opportunity to proactively create an environment that prevents it from becoming a crisis. This is analogous to holistic medicine dealing with how we chose to live and eat, before we develop a disease requiring surgical intervention.

The process that we practice, with the Nonflict way at its core, is called "Nonflict Forum". It brings managers together from the company's different departments to work on the issues that each of them face. These meetings take place on a regular basis, usually monthly, and are unique in that they are held under an environment of confidentiality.

Nonflict Forum meetings also deal with personal issues. We know that when an individual goes through a difficult time in his personal life—if someone he loves is ill, for example—his head and heart cannot truly be at his work. Authentic care for each other, where we let each other know there is always support in the group, creates a high level of trust, and even gratitude.

Over the years we have implemented Nonflict Forum with organizations all over the world.

One of our clients, Chip McElroy was recently quoted in an article on this topic in YPO's Ignite magazine: *"[We have experienced] three years of record, continuous company growth combined with a greater sense of purpose. I would say there has been a dramatic impact to me personally and professionally. We are more focused and disciplined on planning, and even more so on the follow-through. We are also more concise and specific in what we are trying to accomplish together."*

Another CEO, Smoke Wallin revealed, *"Benefits include... creating an environment of sharing and eliminating 'dominant' team members who drown out others. It can not only empower individuals to contribute more but also affect their families as they bring these learnings and experiences home."*

The process of the Nonflict Forum starts with the management committee led by the CEO and attended by key direct reports. Other Forums are formed throughout the organization, where members from different departments in the organization are represented and led by a rotating facilitator.

Here is a glimpse into what many organizations have begun implementing:

The meeting starts with an icebreaker, which is designed to connect and bring us to the moment.

This is followed by a personal introspection focusing on three dimensions:

1. My self
2. My unit or the area to which I belong or lead
3. The total organization

Each shares her experiences, about that period's best success, or sources of pride and most energizing things that is happening or happened, or challenges that sap energy and "keeps me up at night". After everyone in the group has had an uninterrupted turn, each identifies the one issue that he needs to work on that day.

At this point we shift into one-on-one Nonflict way coaching,. This coaching can result in either a resolution in his mind of the challenge or a need for the group's support.

The group decides which issues to process in subsequent meetings, and which of the unresolved issues to work on together. These people become the "presenters".

The first presenter speaks uninterrupted, sharing her answers according to the Nonflict way, and ending with a request for specific area the group can explore with her. The members respond by asking the presenter clarifying and thought-provoking questions.

The next step is group sharing where members either share a similar experience including lessons learned or share how they dealt with similar feelings and situations.

The atmosphere must be one of openness and trust, without giving direct advice or telling the other person what she should or should not do. When someone tells us what we should do, we often resist, as we may feel judged, attacked or belittled.

Each participant then shares "a power reminder" with the presenter. The purpose is to help the presenter recognize the power and assets she already has to overcome the issue at hand.

We finally ask the presenter how she feels, what she's planning to do with the issue and if he wants a 'buddy' to work with her to ensure execution and accountability.

The facilitator closes with the group's assessment and learning, value gained and a reminder of confidentiality.

Group members strongly unite around a new organizational culture of openness, trust, and care for each other's success, which is driven by the modeling of its leaders.

As people see the power of this structured dialogue in Nonflict Forum, many take these principles of communication—and in some cases, even the meeting structure—to use at home with their families. In that case the sharing would be about me, family and friends, school or work.

Implementing Nonflict Forum effectively requires further details than the scope of our book allows. Please do not hesitate to contact us directly at info@millionpeacemakers.org to learn more.

Power Of Empathy—Amir Shares A Memorable Story Of Where It All Began

We had a very powerful meeting around the conflict we hoped to influence. As we talked about the conflict, it felt as if we were accusing one another. We all had a hard time fully understanding what it felt like to live on the other side. Each side felt like it was not seen by the other.

A crucial element was missing—an emotional dimension.

People rationally analyzed the situation but did not fully bring themselves into the room, as they did not share the impact this made on who they were. These individuals led in their communities and impacted their countries, but at that moment, I realized, as a facilitator, that we needed to do something different. In a moment of desperation, I came up with an idea of how to take us to a place of deeper empathy and understanding.

I asked the members to divide into five subgroups. One group would represent the Arab side/world. After 9/11, this group felt great hostility as they traveled around the world but mostly as they traveled to the United States.

The second group was the American group, who were subject to a new feeling of high hostility by the Arab world and felt under attack at that point.

The third group was the Israeli group. Here, we wanted to define the real difference between the settlers in the West Bank and the other Israelis. We decided to go with the more extreme right.

The fourth group was the Palestinians group, different from the Arab world that needed to be represented in that situation. Finally, the fifth group was the rest of the world, looking at this conflict and being influenced by it in a great way.

The idea was to walk in the other groups' shoes. To help understand what it felt like to be a member of each group of these various identities, I asked a few members from each side to coach their new "compatriots" on how it felt to live and experience life from their point of view.

A member from the Arab side represented a settler from the West Bank; an Israeli represented a Palestinian; someone from the Arab world represented an American; and an American represented someone from the Arab world.

The first to speak was a member from the Arab side, who was about to represent the perspective of a settler from the West Bank. As he stood up and started talking, he raised his voice with great force and with extreme eloquence, describing the point of view, the argumentation, and the feelings that were part of the settler's world. Our mouths dropped opened with disbelief. What follows is a bit of what he said:

"This is our land, where we have been here for over 4,000 years. Who are you wandering tribes to claim this land, which has been ours, given to us by God and which has been under our continuous civilization for thousands of years? After the world turned its back on us as the Jewish people, with massacre after massacre, culminating in the Holocaust, this is the only place in the world that we can call our home and homeland, where we feel safe. This is the place where we deserve to defend our presence. We have only this small plot of land, the only place for the Jewish people, and yet you, the Muslim world with hundreds of millions, have twenty-two countries surrounding us. We deserve to have this homeland, and we deserve to be in it, in the place where our ancestors have always been, in all of the land of Israel, which includes the West Bank."

The room was in dramatic silence as he concluded his passionate speech. We realized something very powerful had happened—the other person truly understood us and our pain.

Many times when we are in conflict, we claim clearly that we are not understood. Many times we say, "You don't understand me!" And yet at this point, as we heard this amazing member speak, we realized he truly did know how it felt on the other side.

There was a feeling of depth and connection like never before. Next, an Israeli, representing the Palestinians, stood up. The speaker was an ex-fighter pilot who fought in the Israeli wars, and we all looked at him carefully, especially the Israelis, to see whether he would fully express what it felt like to be a Palestinian.

As he started talking, he chose to represent a young Palestinian being stopped at a road block and seeing his elderly father being questioned in an aggressive way—he felt that his dad was being dis-respected and abused by a young Israeli soldier at the checkpoint. The perspective through the eyes of that young Palestinian brought tears to a few of us, as we realized the pain coming through the sense of humiliation from that setting.

Members of the Arab side became very quiet, as they felt that this was a unique moment, where they were fully understood for their pain.

The next person was an American, who spoke as an Arab. He described the feeling of going through an airport security line for a flight coming into the United States. He described the feeling of humiliation in being profiled and being targeted for a deeper search behind a screen, with a physical examination, in order to verify that he was not carrying a bomb on the flight. As he then described his sense that he was being looked at as a threat and the fear in the eyes of the people who interacted with him, it became clear that all sides were suffering.

Next, an Arab person representing an American stood up. It was clear to see the fear in the eyes of the "American" as he described the experience of living in the United States after 9/11. He said that the Unites States was a nation that represented peace, harmony, and good will, and he could not understand why it had become the target of such hatred and unprovoked killing. He spoke of the sheer terror of not knowing if they would ever be safe again in their own country.

There again was deep silence and reflection in the room. People realized that they were in the presence of human beings who were fully able to understand each other, both on the rational and—much more important—on the emotional level.

Empathy was introduced into the room, and with empathy came a sense of full acceptance of each other as people and a validation of a different point of view. We were then ready to ask ourselves and the others what we could hope for in the future.

What's Next?

Through the extensive use of the Nonflict way workshop we created, we have been so fortunate to witness change in many countries. The training we offer begins with learning effective listening skills and using them to confront individual conflicts. As the course progresses, the participants' skills grow, allowing them to work on larger personal problems. Some of the workshops culminate in working on solutions to conflicts between nations, using a personal perspective. Not only does this allow both the participants and facilitators to experience success using our technique in a variety of scenarios, but it also allows us to feel real empathy in a way that many never have felt—and this is one of the central keys to the success of our method. We have had important and insightful impact using our method across interreligious–based conflicts; in the conflicts between Israelis and the Palestinian/Arab world; between Turks and Greeks; and between Indians and Pakistanis, to name just a few.

We are inspired by the obvious shift from being a victim of conflict to being proactive, using a structured system of dialogue, with the Nonflict way. We are in awe of the consistent power and synergies of groups we have, when they better understand themselves and others. When people realize they are not alone and there is commonality in what's important to them and others, they are capable of co-creating out-of-the-box solutions. In being open, in really listening and understanding, we strengthen our families, our communities, and ourselves.

All it takes is an idea, a little training with the tools in this book, practice, and a vision for us to make a difference.

Please communicate with us at millionpeacemakers.org, and let us know of your successes or challenges.

Acknowledgments

The place where we most practice conflict is home, and as do others, I have my share. I want to thank my parents, Ruth and Aharon Kfir, and my siblings, Anat and Shalom, who have been models in life in dealing with conflict and keeping the family together with harmony and care. My father is a powerful speaker and storyteller, a university professor who has been teaching conflict resolution for sixty years and has been a model in the art of a balanced approach, while finding a place of integration between real and imaginary conflict. My mother has taught us love and care in the family and with friends, practicing my dad's life teaching with us.

To my family—my wife, Sorana; my daughter, Ronnie; and my son, Gil—you have always been the place where this practice meant the most for my well-being and are a source of love and energy in my life.

To Dana de Pietro, Talma Maestro, and Eva and Ofir Kedar—you helped in actualizing the vision. To my friends in the Peace Action Network and the important peace forums we ran together, whose names cannot be mentioned for reasons of confidentiality—you were a catalyst for the development of this methodology and gave me a chance to lead the challenging conflict forums toward a peaceful dialogue. You have shown the power of the action forums in some of the most difficult conflicts around the world.

To Bobby Sager who has been a peacemaker, mentor, and a partner in the journey, inspiring me to pursue the passion for impact in the world.

To the business leaders who have given me an opportunity to develop this methodology and the practice of corporate, social, and personal transformation—the late Anita Roddick and Takis Gerolymatos, Assaf Ben Dov, Chip McElroy, Christian Stammkoetter, Elisa Salinas, Erez Meltzer, Kirill Liseyev, Liat Aronson, Einat Rot, Abhijit Pawar, Kirill Liseyev, Patrick Ghidirim, Ran Poliakine, Ulysses Kyriacopoulos, Yoki Gil, and Norm Asbjornson.

To my friend and partner in making this book a reality, Steve Hecht, thank you for your amazing supportive family and for your passion and push for action and the dream to educate the Nonflict way to the masses.

Thank you all for giving me the opportunity to learn and share.

—Amir

Thanks to my incredible wife, Naomi, for whom I am grateful every single day; my children, all of whom I am so proud of—Yaffa, Alex, William, and Jonathan, who also helped extensively with editing; my special stepkids, Elliot, Gabriel, and Gregory (who came up with the word "Nonflict"); my parents, who get wiser as I get older; my siblings, Clifford and Janice, with whom I got to experience many conflicts growing up yet notwithstanding our very different personalities are learning to see that family is what's really important; Ching, Kallee, and Alicia; Devan Capur, Raj Mitta, Michalis Michael,

Acknowledgments

Sherri Magee, Mike Watson, Greg Milne, Jay Rothman, PhD,Peter Coleman, PhD, Alan McLaren, Dick Simon, Ab Freig, Paul Hayman, Jason Rogers, Catie Ashley, Harvey Beck, Jason, Chloe and Tote Axmith, Nadeem Noordin, Lauren Hofmeister, who've all had direct or indirect influence on the book; my forum mates, past and present, who helped practice group resolution skills; Adrian, Alain, Brian, Dan, Jean, Rod, Johanne, Richard, Marc, Bill and Robert; my religious teachers and mentors, Rabbi Chaim Steinmetz, Father John Walsh, and Imam Zijad Delic, who are working together to help us understand each other (see their blog, faithblender. com); Frederic Latreille, Alex Gauthier, Stephane Ethier, Amal Elsana Alh'jooj, Francesco Lombardo, Stanley and Dominique Dumornay, Lesley Anne Brown, Anne Beliveau, Michelle Bernard, Harry Epstein, Tamisha Harris, Laura Giadorou-Koch, Solmaz Meghadi, Jon Moyal, Nida Nizam, Hanya Omar, Declan Ramsaran, Mark Sadovnick, Jay Shetty, Rod Perry, Vincent Valeri, and Marisa Samek, for sharing your brilliance, passion, and commitment to spreading the Nonflict way through Million Peacemakers; Pascal Bertrand, for your illuminating illustrations; and for putting all of this into print thanks in particular to Marna, Kate, and Allison; and Marissa Madill from Smith Publicity.

And thanks to my new partner in peace, Amir, whom I am proud to call my friend.

Finally, this book is dedicated to all of you Peacemakers who are transforming conflict into Nonflict.

—Steve

26533409R00084

Made in the USA
San Bernardino, CA
20 February 2019